*Love Letters
of Great Women*

Love Letters
of Great Women

Edited by Ursula Doyle

St. Martin's Press · New York

www.stmartins.com

Library of Congress Cataloging-in-Publication Data

Love letters of great women / edited by Ursula Doyle. — 1st U.S. ed.
    p. cm.
Includes bibliographical references.
ISBN 978-0-312-60902-3
1. Love-letters. I. Doyle, Ursula.
PN6140.L7L64 2009
808.86'3543—dc22

                                                              2009037415

First published in Great Britain by Macmillan, an imprint of Pan Macmillan Ltd.
First U.S. Edition: November 2009

10 9 8 7 6 5 4 3 2 1

To the memory of four great women:
AD and MIS; AD and ND

Contents

Introduction

When *Love Letters of Great Men*, this volume's predecessor, was published, it gave rise to a small discussion about whether or not people write love letters any more. The consensus seemed to be that today's instant communication has supplanted words on paper, and it was viewed as even more improbable that a *man* would nowadays put himself out to such an extent as to write a letter (and then post it). But it seemed that what people (and it has to be said mainly women) were lamenting was not the usurping of the love letter by text messaging or email, but rather the passing of an age when men actually talked about their feelings rather than grunting from the sofa. There was an appetite for reading the romantic (and not so romantic) outpourings of various men from history, perhaps not because of who those men were, but because such outpourings are thin on the ground today – in any form.

Those letters, as I wrote at the time, varied enormously in style, sentiment and (sad to say) sincerity – it did sometimes seem as though some Great Men wrote with an eye to posterity, or believed that a love letter was just another vehicle for demonstrating their creative brilliance. Compiling this volume has been a very different reading experience. For the Great Men of history, the matter of who they loved and who they might marry was but one aspect of their lives; their Greatness rested on their achievements in other spheres: scientific discovery, exploration, conquest, political triumph, artistic endeavour. These avenues were not open to most women until shockingly recently, and it is a sad fact that the Greatness of many of the women in this collection rests either on who they married or to whom they gave birth; their connection with their illustrious spouses or off-spring was the only reason their letters were preserved at all. For many of the women here, marriage would determine their entire destiny. I cannot (and of course would not) claim that women are more often sincere than men, or less capable of dissimulation and posturing; the point is that affairs of the heart could irrevocably alter the course of a woman's life in a way they did not a man's. It is hard to imagine any of the Great Men writing, as Lady Mary Wortley Montagu did to her beloved before eloping with him against her father's wishes in 1712, 'I tremble for what we are doing. Are you sure you will love me for ever? Shall we never repent? I fear, and I hope.' For a woman, the consequences of making the wrong decision, of playing the wrong hand, could be nothing short of disastrous.

There are women here, of course, who did flout convention, disobeyed their families and fought to take control of their lives. But in the main these women were exceptionally brilliant, independently wealthy, or both. Which is to take nothing away from their achievements; it is simply worth noting that the bar to success for women was set almost impossibly high. And of course there are other women in the collection who were actively encouraged and helped by the wonderful men they married – Abigail Adams and Isabella Beeton, for instance, seem to have had husbands who, hearteningly, wanted them to succeed at all they did.

There are sad stories here – not only of the love affairs that ended badly, but also of the danger and heartbreak women endured in so many aspects of their lives, from their powerlessness and lack of education and economic independence to the deadly hazards presented by childbirth and the likelihood of those children dying very young. Antibiotics and the vote changed everything – at least in the more economically developed world (it is worth noting the terrible statistic from the UN that of the 536,000 maternal deaths each year, 99 per cent now occur in less economically developed countries). This doesn't feel like a 'You've come a long way, baby' moment, but it is sometimes good to remember how much progress women have made since Mary Wollstonecraft wrote her *Vindication of the Rights of Women* in 1790.

What shines through this collection for me is the resilience of these women in the face of what seem insuperable difficulties: their bravery, their stoicism, their wit, their charm and their generosity. The love written here comes in many forms – tolerant, deluded, ambiguous, ambitious, selfish, erotic, chaste and mad – but love it is, and a legacy to cherish.

Ursula Doyle, London, 2009

'I used to look at all these daft girls, marrying the first fellow they thought they could live with. And I suppose I was waiting for the fellow I couldn't live without.'

Nora Doyle, 1917–2007

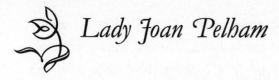

Lady Joan Pelham

This 1399 letter from Lady Pelham to her husband, Sir John, was written from their home at Pevensey Castle in East Sussex. Sir John Pelham was away, helping Henry Bolingbroke to rally troops for what became a successful attempt to wrest the throne from Richard II. Pevensey was besieged by her husband's enemies; Lady Pelham, without wishing to make a fuss, is enquiring whether he might be returning soon.

To Sir John Pelham, (15 July?) 1399

My dear Lord,
I recommend me to your high lordship, with heart and body and all my poor might. And with all this I thank you as my dear Lord, dearest and best beloved of all earth lords. I say for me, and thank you, my dear Lord, with all this that I said before for your comfortable letter that you sent me from Pontefract, that came to me on Mary Magdalen's day; for by my troth I was never so glad as when I heard by your letter ye were strong enough with the Grace of God to keep you from the malice of your enemies. And, dear Lord, if it like to your high Lordship that as soon as ye might that I might

hear of your gracious speed, which God Almighty continue and increase. And, my dear Lord, if it like you to know *my* fare, I am here laid by in a manner of a siege with the County of Sussex, Surrey and a great parcel of Kent, so that I may not go out nor no victuals get me, but with much hazard. Wherefore, my dear, if it like you by the advice of your wise counsel for to set remedy to the salvation of your castle and withstand the malice of the shires aforesaid. And also that ye be fully informed of the great malice-workers in these shires which have so despitefully wrought to you, and to your castle, to your men, and to your tenants; for this country have they wasted for a great while.

Farewell, my dear Lord! the Holy Trinity keep you from your enemies, and soon send me good tidings of you. Written at Pevensey, in the castle, on St Jacob's day last past, by your own poor J. Pelham. To my true Lord.

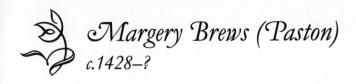

Margery Brews (Paston)
c.1428–?

The Pastons were a prominent Norfolk family of the late medieval period who left behind a treasure trove of letters covering four generations, which paint a vivid picture of life at the time. The letters below, from Margery Brews to John Paston, written in 1476, are sometimes described as the oldest love letters in the English language but in fact they are more businesslike than they might at first appear. Their primary topic is the ongoing negotiations over the size of Margery's dowry, which the Paston family considered too small. Margery and John did eventually marry in 1477.

To John Paston
Sent from Topcroft, February 1476

Unto my right well-beloved Valentine, John Paston, Esq., be this Bill delivered, &c.

Right reverend and worshipful, and my right well-beloved Valentine, I recommend me unto you, full heartily desiring to hear of your welfare, which I beseech Almighty God long for to preserve unto his pleasure and your heart's desire.

And if it please you to hear of my welfare, I am not in good heele of body nor of heart, nor shall I be till I hear from you.

For there wottys [knows] no creature what pain that I endure,
And for to be dead, I dare it not dyscur

And my lady my mother hath laboured the matter to my father full diligently, but she can no more get than ye know of, for the which God knoweth I am full sorry. But if that ye love me, as I trust verily that ye do, ye will not leave me therefore; for if that ye had not half the livelihood that ye have, for to do the greatest labour that any woman alive might, I would not forsake you.

And if ye command me to keep me true wherever I go,
I wis I will de all my might you to love, and never no mo.
And if my friends say that I do amiss,
They shall not me let so for to do,
Mine heart me bids evermore to love you
Truly over all earthly thing,
And if they be never so wrath,
I trust it shall be better in time coming.

No more to you at this time, but the Holy Trinity have you in keeping; and I beseech you that this bill be not seen of none earthly creature save only yourself, &c.

And this letter was endited at Topcroft, with fully heavy heart, &c.

By your own

Margery Brews

To John Paston

I thank you with all my heart for the letter you sent me . . . from which I know for certain that you intend to come . . . shortly, with no other errand or business except to bring to a conclusion the business between my father and you. I would be the happiest one alive if only the business might come to fruition . . . And if you come and the business comes to nothing, then I will be even sorrier and full of sadness.

As for myself, I have done and endured in the business as much as I know how or am able to, God knows. And I want you to understand clearly that my father refuses to part with any more money than one hundred [pounds] and fifty marks in this business, which is far from fulfilling your wishes.

For which reason, if you could be content with that amount and my poor person, I would be the happiest maid on earth. And if you do not consider yourself satisfied with that, or believe that you could get more money, as I have understood from you before, good, faithful and loving Valentine, do not take the trouble to visit anymore on this business. Rather let it be finished and never spoken of again, on condition that I may be your faithful friend and petitioner for the duration of my life.

No more to you now, but may Almighty Jesus preserve you, in both body and soul.

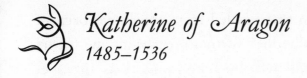

Katherine of Aragon
1485–1536

Katherine of Aragon was born at the palace at Alcalá de Henares, north-east of Madrid, on 16 December 1485, the daughter of Ferdinand of Aragon and Isabella of Castile. Isabella was determined that her daughters should have a good education based on Catholic principles. Katherine's knowledge of Latin, European languages and classical literature was widely admired, and she was extremely devout.

When the princess was only two, Henry VII of England proposed a match between Katherine and his eldest son, Arthur, Prince of Wales, who was a year younger than the prospective bride. After negotiations lasting more than ten years, the princess arrived in Plymouth in October 1501, and the marriage between Katherine of Aragon and Arthur, Prince of Wales, was solemnized in St Paul's on 14 November.

By the following April, at the age of fifteen, Arthur was dead. The Spanish immediately expressed an interest in Katherine marrying Henry, the new Prince of Wales. Henry VII was at first amenable, but negotiations dragged on in England, in Spain and in Rome (a dispensation was needed from the Pope, because Henry was Katherine's former brother-in-law) for six years. Katherine remained in London as dowager Princess of Wales; she was homesick and short of money, frequently complaining to her father about the tight-fisted behaviour of Henry VII. By March 1509, she was begging to be allowed to return to Spain and enter a convent. Henry and Katherine were finally married in June 1509, just weeks after Henry succeeded to the throne.

The length of the marriage – more than twenty years – is often eclipsed by what followed; Henry's five subsequent marriages took place over ten tumultuous years from 1533. It also appears that the pair were content for much of their married life, although Katherine's many miscarriages and stillbirths must have taken their toll – her only surviving child was Princess Mary, born in 1516. Katherine exists in popular myth as a dumpy, depressed religious maniac, with her rosary beads, broken English and unglamorous gynaecological problems, but the evidence suggests that Henry respected his wife to the extent that she took charge of affairs of state in his absence – notwithstanding her unshakeable belief that a wife's Christian duty was to obey her husband in all things. The first letter below was written while Henry was off fighting the French; Katherine had successfully repelled a Scottish invasion led by James IV, and the king himself had been left dead in the field. She gleefully writes of sending Henry the dead monarch's coat, implying that she would rather have liked to send his body, but her squeamish English courtiers would not allow it.

The rupture between Henry and Katherine was a more complicated business than one might be led to believe from its numerous portrayals in fiction, where it comes about through Henry's boredom with his ageing wife and his enslavement by the bewitching Anne Boleyn. If these were factors, there were several others, including the dwindling importance of the alliance with Spain, and Henry's obsession with producing a male heir. There is no doubt, however, that his treatment of Katherine was horrible. He put her through a humiliating trial concerning the consummation of her marriage to his brother, and after the annulment kept her apart from her beloved daughter, who he had proclaimed illegitimate.

After Anne Boleyn was installed as queen, Katherine was sent to the provinces, first to Huntingdon and then to Cambridgeshire. She refused to recognize Anne's title, refused to accept her own of princess dowager, and refused to sign an oath recognizing

Anne's children as the legitimate successors to Henry. She died in 1536, steadfastly proclaiming that her marriage to Henry was valid, that she was queen, and that she continued to love her husband. Her final letter to him, the second below, is heartbreaking: 'Lastly, do I vow, that mine eyes desire you above all things.' Henry and Anne marked her death by dressing in yellow and parading their daughter, the baby Princess Elizabeth, around the court.

To Henry VIII, 16 September 1513

Sir, My Lord Howard hath sent me a letter open to your Grace, within one of mine, by the which you shall see at length the great Victory that our Lord hath sent your subjects in your absence; and for this cause there is no need herein to trouble your Grace with long writing, but, to my thinking, this battle hath been to your Grace and all your realm the greatest honor that could be, and more than you should win all the crown of France; thanked be God of it, and I am sure your Grace forgetteth not to do this, which shall be cause to send you many more such great victories, as I trust he shall do. My husband, for hastiness, with Rougecross I could not send your Grace the piece of the King of Scots coat which John Glynn now brings. In this your Grace shall see how I keep my promise, sending you for your banners a king's coat. I thought to send himself unto you, but our Englishmens' hearts would not suffer it. It should have been better for him to have been in peace than have this reward. All that God sends is for the best.

My Lord of Surrey, my Henry, would fain know your pleasure in the burying of the King o Scots' body, for he has written to me so. With the next messenger your Grace's pleasure may be herein known. And with this I make an end, praying God to send you home shortly, for without this no joy here can be accomplished; and for the same I pray, and now go to Our Lady of Walsingham that I promised so long ago to see. At Woburn the 16th of September.

I send your Grace herein a bill found in a Scotsman's purse of such things as the French King sent to the said King of Scots to make war against you, beseeching you to send Mathew hither as soon as this messenger comes to bring me tidings from your Grace.

Your humble wife and true servant, Katherine.

To Henry VIII, 1535

My Lord and Dear Husband,

I commend me unto you. The hour of my death draweth fast on, and my case being such, the tender love I owe you forceth me, with a few words, to put you in remembrance of the health and safeguard of your soul, which you ought to prefer before all worldly matters, and before the care and tendering of your own body, for the which you have cast me into many miseries and yourself into many cares.

For my part I do pardon you all, yea, I do wish and devoutly pray God that He will also pardon you.

For the rest I commend unto you Mary, our daughter, beseeching you to be a good father unto her, as I heretofore desired. I entreat you also, on behalf of my maids, to give them marriage-portions, which is not much, they being but three. For all my other servants, I solicit a year's pay more than their due, lest they should be unprovided for.

Lastly, do I vow, that mine eyes desire you above all things.

Anne Boleyn
c.1500–36

Anne Boleyn was the daughter of Thomas Boleyn, Earl of Ormond, and Elizabeth Howard, the daughter of Thomas Howard, Duke of Norfolk. Thomas Boleyn was enormously ambitious for his three children, of whom Anne was the second, and when at the age of thirteen she was offered a position as a lady-in-waiting at the court of Margaret of Austria in Brussels, he saw it as an unmissable opportunity. Margaret's was among the most prestigious courts of Europe, and would equip Anne for the ultimate prize, a place at the court of Katherine of Aragon. But shortly after her arrival in Brussels, the diplomatic situation changed, and Anne was moved to France, where she entered the service of Claude, the queen. The two became close, and Anne acquired a polish and glamour that was immediately apparent when she returned to the English court in 1521 – accomplished, tasteful, witty and beautifully dressed, she was absolutely unlike her contemporaries.

The next step for Anne was marriage, but several avenues of enquiry came to nothing, possibly because in her father's eyes the suitors on offer were insufficiently grand. And then, in 1526 or thereabouts, Anne caught the eye of Henry VIII. The king was ready for a new mistress, having recently dispensed with the services of Mary, Anne's sister. But it so happened that the vacancy coincided with Henry's growing conviction, in the absence of a male heir, that his marriage to Katherine had never been valid.

The annulment of Henry and Katherine's marriage and his subsequent marriage to Anne played out over the next six years. The political and religious fallout was huge, and led ultimately to Henry's break with Rome and the establishment of the Church of England. The couple were finally married in January 1533, when Anne was just pregnant; Princess Elizabeth was born on 7 September.

It was not a disaster for Anne that her first child was a girl; she was still young. But a miscarriage in August 1534 did not augur well, and she did not conceive again until the autumn of 1535. In January 1536, Katherine died, which came as a relief to Henry and Anne, who knew how much support she and her daughter, Mary, retained in the country at large; this relief was short-lived, as Anne had another miscarriage at the end of the same month. Still, the situation might have been salvageable, had it not been for Anne's falling out with the Lord Chancellor, Thomas Cromwell, previously a key ally, and for important diplomatic negotiations being scuppered by Henry's insistence that powerful European monarchs recognize Anne as his lawful wife.

Anne had to go, and Thomas Cromwell arranged it. A mere divorce would not suffice; Anne and her faction had to be permanently dispatched. So Cromwell cooked up a selection of terrible charges, accusing her not only of incestuous relations with her brother George, but adultery with four other men of her circle. All were arrested and taken to the Tower.

After trials of non-existent legality, George Boleyn and his co-accused were executed on 17 May 1536, and that afternoon the Archbishop of Canterbury declared Anne and Henry's marriage null and void on the grounds of Henry's previous association with Mary Boleyn (which rather begs the question of how an unmarried Anne managed to commit the alleged adultery). On 19 May, Anne was executed on Tower Green by a swordsman brought over from France in order to spare her the axe. It was less than six months since the death of Katherine of Aragon. On 30 May Henry married Jane Seymour, one of Anne's ladies-in-waiting.

The letter below, dated 6 May, exists only as a copy, and so its authenticity has not been established.

To Henry VIII, 6 May 1536

Sir,

Your graces displeasure, and my Imprisonment are things so Strange unto me, and what to write or what to excuse, I am altogether ignorant, whereas you send unto me (willing me to confess a truth and so to obtain your favour) by such a one, whom you know to be my ancient professed enemy, I no sooner received this message by him, than I right conceived your meaning; and if as you say confessing a truth in deed, may procure my safety, I shall with all willingness and duty perform your Command; but let not your grace ever imagine that your poor wife, will ever be brought to acknowledge fault where not so much as a thought thereof proceeded, and to speak a truth, never prince had wife more Loyal in all duty, and in all true affection, than you have ever found in Anne Boleyn, with which name and place I could willingly have contented myself, if so god and your graces pleasure had been pleased. Neither did I at any time so far forget my self in my exaltation, or received queenship, but that I always looked for such an alteration as now I find, for the ground of my preferment being on no surer foundation than your graces fancy, the least alteration, I knew was fit and sufficient to draw that fancy to some other subject.

You have chosen me from a low estate to be your Queen and Companion, far beyond my desert or desire, if then you found me worthy of such honour, good your grace, let not any light fancy or bad counsel of my enemies, withdraw your princely favour from me, neither let that stain, that unworthy stain of a disloyal heart towards your grace ever cast so foul a blot on your most dutiful wife and the infant princess your daughter; try me good king, but let me have a lawful trial, and let not my sworn enemies sit as my accusers and judges; yea let me receive an open trial, for my truth shall fear no open shames; then shall you see either my innocency cleared, your suspicion and conscience satisfied, the ignominy and slander of the world stopped, or my guilt openly declared; so that what so ever God or you may determine of me, your grace may be freed from an open censure, and my offence being so lawfully proved, your grace is at liberty, both before God and man, not only to execute worthy punishment on me as an unfaithful wife, but to follow your affection already settled on that party, for whose sake I come now as I am, whose name I could some good while sith have pointed unto your grace, being not ignorant of my suspicion therein.

But if you have already determined of me, and that not only my death but an infamous slander must bring you the enjoying your desired happiness, then I desire of God that he will pardon your greater sin herein, and likewise my enemies, the instruments thereof; and if he will not call you to a straight account for your unprincely and cruel usage of me, at his general Judgement Seat, where both you and my self must shortly appear, and in whose right judgement I doubt not (what so ever the world may think of me), mine innocence shall be openly known, and sufficiently cleared;

my last and only request shall be, that my self may only bear the burthen of your graces displeasure, and that it may not touch the innocent souls of those poor gentlemen whom as I understand are likewise in straight imprisonment for my sake; If ever I have found favour in your sight; if ever the name of Anne Boleyn have been pleasing to your ears let me obtain this last request. And I will so leave to trouble your grace any further, with my earnest prayers to the Trinity to have your grace in his good keeping, and to direct you in all your actions. From my doleful prison in the Tower this 6 of May,

    Yr most loyal and faithful wife

    A.B.

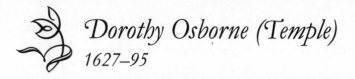

Dorothy Osborne (Temple)
1627–95

Dorothy Osborne was from a family who took the royalist part during England's civil war; her father, Sir Peter Osborne, was the lieutenant-governor of the Channel island of Guernsey. After the outbreak of the civil war, her mother, Lady Dorothy, took her children from their home in Bedfordshire to St Malo in France to be near her husband, who was besieged in Castle Cornet on Guernsey. In 1644, having got herself into debt sending provisions to Sir Peter, Lady Dorothy brought the family back to England, where they resided temporarily in Chelsea at the home of her brother, as Bedfordshire was in the hands of parliamentarian forces. Two of Dorothy's own brothers were killed in the civil war, the second in 1646, the year Sir Peter was forced to retreat from Guernsey and made for St Malo. It was on a voyage out to see her father that Dorothy met Sir William Temple, a young man who was embarking on a continental tour, having left Cambridge without taking his degree.

A lengthy and intermittent courtship ensued. Dorothy's father and her brothers were implacably opposed to the marriage; the Osborne finances had been severely depleted by the war, and they had hoped Dorothy would find a rich husband. In 1648 Sir William departed once more for the Continent, and in 1651, after the lovers managed to meet in London, Dorothy's family returned to Bedfordshire. There she was presented with endless suitable young men, all of whom she rejected. This was when the correspondence between the lovers began in earnest; seventy-seven letters from Dorothy to Sir William survive (she destroyed all but one of Sir William's to her). She had to circumvent the close surveillance of her brother Henry, which meant that her letters had to be smuggled out of the house. It wasn't until 1654, after the death of Dorothy's father, that the two were married, although the opposition of her family was unabated. Dorothy suffered a disfiguring and almost fatal attack of smallpox a month before the wedding.

The couple settled initially in Ireland, where they had eight or nine children (at least six died in infancy, but the records are unclear). In 1665, Sir William was appointed ambassador to the Netherlands, where they remained until 1671. Dorothy and Sir William played a behind-the-scenes role in brokering the marriage of William of Orange and Mary Stuart, the daughter of the Duke of York, who jointly ruled England, Scotland and Ireland from 1689. Dorothy and Mary remained confidantes until Mary's death in 1694.

Dorothy died in 1695 at Moor Park, an estate in Surrey that Sir William had bought for their retirement. She was buried in Westminster Abbey. Her vivacious and witty letters were published in various editions from 1836, which is when her literary reputation was secured.

To Sir William Temple, no date

There are a great many ingredients must go to the making me happy in a husband. First, as my cousin Franklin says, our humours must agree; and to do that he must have that kind of breeding that I have had, and used that kind of company. That is, he must not be so much a country gentleman as to understand nothing but hawks and dogs, and be fonder of either than his wife; nor of the next sort of them whose aim reaches no further than to be Justice of the Peace, and once in his life High Sheriff, who reads no book but Statutes, and studies nothing but how to make a speech interlarded with Latin that may amaze his disagreeing poor neighbours, and fright them rather than persuade them into quietness. He must not be a thing that began the world in a free school, was sent from thence to the university, and is at his furthest when he reaches the Inns of Court, has no acquaintances but those of his form in these places, speaks the French he has picked out of old laws, and admires nothing but the stories he has heard of the revels that were kept there before his time. He must not be a town gallant neither, that lives in a tavern and an ordinary, that cannot imagine how an hour should be spent without company unless it be in sleeping, that makes court to all the women he sees, thinks they believe him, and laughs and is laughed at equally. Nor a travelled Monsieur whose head is all feather inside and outside, than can talk of nothing but dancing and duets, and has courage enough to wear slashes when every one else dies with cold to see him. He must not be a fool of no sort, nor peevish, nor ill-natured, nor proud, nor covetous; and to all this must be added, that he must love me and I him as much as we are capable of loving. Without all this, his fortune, though never so great, would not satisfy me; and with it, a very moderate one would keep me from ever repenting my disposal.

To Sir William Temple, no date

'Twill be pleasinger to you, I am sure, to tell how fond I am of your lock. Well, in earnest now, and setting aside all compliments, I never saw finer hair, nor of a better colour; but cut no more on't, I would not have it spoiled for the world. If you love me, be careful on't. I am combing, and curling, and kissing this lock all day, and dreaming on't all night. The ring, too, is very well, only a little of the biggest. Send me a tortoise one that is a little less than that I sent for a pattern. I would not have the rule so absolutely true without exception that hard hairs be ill-natured, for then I should be so. But I can allow that all soft hairs are good, and so are you, or I am deceived as much as you are if you think I do not love you enough. Tell me, my dearest, am I? You will not be if you think I am

Yours.

Nell Gwyn
1651?–87

Nell Gwyn is the most celebrated of the (many) mistresses of King Charles II. Almost nothing is known of her early life, although her detractors liked to spread stories that she was variously a herring-seller, a cinder-sweeper and a servant in a brothel. She is popularly believed to have started out in the theatre selling oranges in 1663; Samuel Pepys first saw her acting at Drury Lane in December 1666.

Nell had liaisons with more than one aristocrat before and after she met the king (the letter below is to Lawrence Hyde, later the Earl of Rochester, who was at The Hague on diplomatic business in May and June 1678). She became Charles II's mistress in 1668 or 1669, and bore him a son, Charles, in May 1670. That summer, a grand house was leased for her in Pall Mall ('pel mel', below), acknowledging her position as a (sadly not 'the') royal mistress, and a second son, James, was born there in 1671. Nell lobbied hard for titles for her boys, and in 1676 Charles was given the surname Beauclerk and created Baron Heddington and Earl of Burford.

Nell had influential friends at court, but also enemies who made no secret of their contempt for her low birth, disreputable former occupation, high spirits and lack of social graces. Her chief enemy was another of the king's mistresses, Louise de Kéroualle, Duchess of Portsmouth, who also happened to be French, Catholic and deeply unpopular with the public. One story has Nell's coach surrounded by an angry mob who believed it to belong to the duchess; they were placated only when Nell stuck her head out of the window and cheerfully announced, 'Pray, good people, be silent, I am the Protestant whore.'

Charles II died in 1685; his last words are reputed to have been, 'Let not poor Nelly starve.' His successor, James II, gave her a generous pension, and she died at Pall Mall in 1687. As befits her reputation for charity, she left £100 to the debtors of her parish and £20 a year to release debtors from prison every Christmas day, as well as £50 to poor Catholics, 'for showing my charity to those who differ from me in Religeon'. In his memoirs Gilbert Burnet, the bishop and historian, described her as the 'indiscreetest and wildest creature that ever was in court', which may explain the longevity of her relationship with a king renowned for his love of a good time.

To Lawrence Hyde, c.1678

Pray dear Mr. Hide forgive me for not writeing to you efore now for the reasone is I have bin sick thre months & sinse I have recovered I have had nothing to intertaine you withal nor have nothing now worth writing but that I can holde no longer to let you know I never had ben in any companie without drinking your health for I loue yo with all my soule. The pel mel is now to me a dismal plase since, I have utterly lost Sr Car Scrope [Sir Carr Scrope, a wit of Charles II's circle] never to be recoured agane for he tould me he could not live allwayes at this rate & so begune to be a little uncivil, which I could not sufer from an ugly *baux garscon*. Ms Knights [a singer, and rival for Charles II's affections] Lady mothers dead & she has put up a scutchin [escutcheon] no bigger then my Lady Grins scunchis [escutcheon]. My lord Rochester [John Wilmot, the scandalous poet, who died two years later] is gon in the cuntrei. Mr Savil [Henry Savile, future Vice-Chamberlain] has got a misfortune, but is upon recovery & is to mary an hairres [heiress], who I thinke wont have an ill time ont if he holds up his thumb. My lord of Dorset [a former protector of Nell's] apiers wonse in thre munths, for he drinkes aile with Shadwell [Thomas Shadwell, poet and another of Charles II's boon companions] & Mr Haris [Joseph Harris, actor] at the Dukes house all day long. My Lord Burford [Nell's son by the king] remembers his sarvis to you. my Lord Bauclaire [Beauclerk, Nell's second son by the king] is goeing into france. We are goeing to supe with the king at whithall & my lady Harvie. the King remembers his sarvis to you. now lets talke of state affairs, for we never carried things so cunningly as now for we don't know whether we shall have peace or war, but I am for war and for no other reason but that you may come home. I have a thousand merry conseets, but I cant make her write um [possibly Nell is dictating this letter, and 'her' refers to the person taking the dictation, although the standard of spelling and grammar suggests perhaps Nell should have looked elsewhere for a secretary] & therefore you must take the will for the deed. god bye. Your most loueing obedunt faithfull & humbel sarvant E. [Eleanor] G.

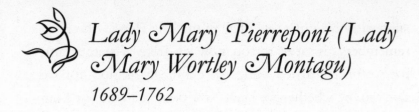

Lady Mary Pierrepont (Lady Mary Wortley Montagu)
1689–1762

Mary Pierrepont was the eldest child of Evelyn Pierrepont, later the first duke of Kingston-upon-Hull, and Lady Mary Feilding. Her mother died in 1692, having given birth to three more children; the siblings were then brought up by their paternal grandmother. When Mary was nine her grandmother died, and care of the children passed to her father. In later years Mary described herself as having 'stolen' her education in the library of his Nottinghamshire mansion, Thoresby Hall.

One of Mary's closest friends as a young woman was Anne Wortley, with whom she regularly corresponded. When Anne died in 1710, the correspondence was taken up by her brother, Edward Wortley Montagu, who soon asked her father's permission for Mary's hand. Permission was not granted because Pierrepont insisted on the entailment of Wortley Montagu's estate on his hypothetical first-born son, a practice with which Edward profoundly disagreed.

In August 1712, with Mary coming under increasing pressure from her father to marry the unsatirisably named Clotworthy Skeffington, the heir to an Irish peerage, Edward and Mary eloped. They were married on 23 August 1712, and the letters below date from the fretful run-up to their wedding. Mary's anxiety at the gamble she was taking is clear, and for the rest of her life she remained deeply grateful to her husband for marrying her without a dowry.

For the first two years of their marriage the couple lived in the country, and Mary gave birth to a son, also Edward, in May 1713. She was already writing poems and criticism, and became the first woman to have a contribution accepted by the *Spectator* magazine. In 1715, the Wortley Montagus moved to London and became important figures at the court of George I. Mary struck up friendships with politicians and members of the literati, including John Gay and Alexander Pope, who fell in love with her. In December that year, she barely survived a severe bout of smallpox, which left her permanently scarred.

In August 1716 Edward Wortley Montagu was posted as a diplomat to Constantinople in Turkey. The couple travelled out overland, the journey lasting about six months; Mary wrote many letters describing the fearsome undertaking, and kept copies with the intention of working them up into a book. In Turkey, she immersed herself in the local literature, culture, customs and religion, until her husband was unexpectedly recalled to London in July 1718, six months after Mary had given birth to a daughter.

After their return to England, Edward, frequently away on business in Yorkshire, bought houses in Twickenham and in Covent Garden, where Mary spent most of her time writing, gardening and overseeing the education of her daughter; she also wrote a series of poems about the oppression of women and edited her travel letters. She began a vicious feud with her former friend and admirer Alexander Pope, the reasons for which remain obscure. Her most important and lasting act during this time was to introduce the smallpox inoculation to England. She had come across it in Turkey, where inoculation with the live virus was a common practice. She had her son inoculated while they were there, and with a smallpox epidemic raging in England in 1721 she persuaded a doctor to inoculate her daughter. Soon, many of her acquaintances who had lost relatives to the disease were having their children inoculated too, and the practice became both increasingly widespread and endlessly controversial. Mary's evangelizing on behalf of inoculation led to her denunciation in the newspapers and even from the pulpit as an unnatural mother who risked the lives of her children to prove her crackpot theory, but Mary remained steadfast and encouraged other mothers to have their offspring inoculated against the disease that had nearly claimed her own life.

For the rest of her days Mary lived almost entirely apart from her husband. In 1736, she became infatuated with a brilliant young Venetian writer, Francesco Algarotti, and travelled to Italy in the hope of their having some kind of life together. For the next few years her movements were dictated by his whereabouts, and she spent time in Rome, Naples, Florence, Venice and Turin; she also lived for four years in Avignon, and for ten years in the Venetian province of Brescia, where she was more or less held captive by an upper-class bandit and thug named Ugolino Palazzi, who stole all her jewels and the title deeds to the property she had bought. When she returned to London in 1762, she had been abroad for the best part of thirty years; she died in Mayfair in August of that year, and is buried in the Grosvenor Chapel in South Audley Street.

Lady Mary Wortley Montagu undoubtedly had the capacity to become a great writer, but her work was so diverse in form – letters, journals, polemics, plays, poems, essays – and scattered in so many different places that its evaluation is still far from complete.

To Edward Wortley Montagu, 25 April 1710

I have this minute received your two letters. I know not how to direct you, whether to London or the country. 'Tis very likely you will never receive this. I hazard a great deal if it falls into other hands, and I write for all that.

I wish with all my soul I thought as you do; I endeavour to convince myself by your arguments, and am sorry my reason is so obstinate, not to be deluded into an opinion, that 'tis impossible a man can esteem a woman. I suppose I should then be very easy at your thoughts of me; I should thank you for the wit and beauty you give me, and not be angry at the follies and weaknesses; but, to my infinite affliction, I can believe neither one nor t'other.

One part of my character is not so good, nor t'other as bad as you fancy it. Should we ever live together, you would be disappointed both ways; you would find an easy equality of temper you do not expect, and a thousand faults you do not imagine.

You think, if you married me, I should be passionately fond of you one month, and of somebody else the next. Neither would happen. I can esteem, I can be a friend, but I don't know whether I can love. Expect all that is complaisant and easy, but never what is fond, in me. You judge a very wrong of my heart when you suppose me capable of views of interest, and that anything could oblige me to flatter anybody.

Was I the most indigent creature in the world, I should answer you as I do now, without adding or diminishing. I am incapable of art, and 'tis because I will not be capable of it. Could I deceive one minute, I should never regain my own good opinion, and who could bear to live with one they despised?

If you can resolve to live with a companion that will have all the deference due to your superiority of good sense, and that your proposals can be agreeable to those on whom I depend, I have nothing to say against them.

As to travelling, 'tis what I should do with great pleasure, and could easily quit London upon your account, but a retirement in the country is not so disagreeable to me, as I know a few months would make it tiresome to you. Where people are tied for life, 'tis their mutual interest not to grow weary of one another. If I had all the personal charms that I want, a face is too slight a foundation for happiness. You would be soon tired with seeing every day the same thing, where you saw nothing else. You would have leisure to remark all the defects, which would increase in proportion as the novelty lessened, which is always a great charm. I should have the displeasure of seeing a coldness, which tho' I could not reasonably blame you for, being involuntary, yet it would render me uneasy, and the more because I know a love may be revived, which absence, inconstancy or even infidelity has extinguished, but there is no returning from a degôut given by satiety.

I should not choose to live in a crowd. I could be very well pleased to be in London without making a great figure or seeing above eight or nine agreeable people. Apartments, table, etc. are things that never come into my head. But I will never think of any thing without the consent of my family, and advise you not to fancy a happiness in entire solitude, which you would find only fancy.

Make no answer to this. If you can like me on my own terms, 'tis not to me you must make your proposals. If not, to what purpose is our correspondence?

However, preserve me your friendship, which I think of with a great deal of pleasure and some vanity. If ever you see me married, I flatter my self you'll see a conduct you would not be sorry your wife should imitate.

To Edward Wortley Montagu, Friday night, 15 August 1712

I tremble for what we are doing. Are you sure you will love me for ever? Shall we never repent? I fear, and I hope. I foresee all that will happen on this occasion. I shall incense my family to the highest degree. The generality of the world will blame my conduct, and the relations and friends of ———— will invent a thousand stories of me. In this letter (which I am fond of) you promise me all that I wish. – Since I writ so far, I received your Friday letter. I will be only yours, and I will do what you please.

Postscript: You shall hear from me again tomorrow, not to contradict but to give some directions. My resolution is taken – love me and use me well.

Saturday morning, 16 August 1712

I writ you a letter last night in some passion. I begin to fear again; I own myself a coward. – You made no reply to one part of my letter concerning my fortune. I am afraid you flatter yourself that my father may be at length reconciled and brought to reasonable terms. I am convinced by what I have often heard him say, speaking of other cases like this, he never will. The fortune he has engaged to give with me was settled, on my brother's marriage, on my sister and myself, but in such a manner that it was left in his power to give it all to either of us, or divide it as he thought fit. He has given it all to me. Nothing remains for my sister but the free bounty of my father from what he can save, which notwithstanding the greatness of his estate may be very little. Possibly after I have disobliged him so much, he may be glad to have her so easily provided for, with money already raised, especially if he has a design to marry himself, as I hear.

I do not speak this that you should not endeavour to come to terms with him, if you please, but I am fully persuaded it will be to no purpose. He will have a very good answer to make, that I suffered this match to proceed, that I made him a very silly figure in it, that I have let him spend

£400 in wedding clothes, all which I saw without saying any thing. When I first pretended to oppose this match, he told me he was sure I had some other design in my head. I denied it with truth, but you see how little appearance there is of that truth. He proceeded with telling me that he would never enter into treaty with another man, etc., and that I should be sent immediately into the north, to stay there, and when he died he would only leave me an annuity of £400.

I had not courage to stand this vein, and I submitted to what he pleased. He will now object against me, why, since I intended to marry in this manner, I did not persist in my first resolution? that it would have been as easy for me to run away from Thoresby as from hence, and to what purpose did I put him and the gentleman I was to marry for Expense etc.? He will have a thousand plausible reasons for being irreconcilable, and 'tis very probable the world will be on his side. – Reflect now for the last time in what manner you must take me. I shall come to you with only a night-gown and petticoat, and this is all you will get with me.

I have told a lady of my friends what I intend to do. You will think her a very good friend when I tell you she has proffered to lend us her house, if we would come there the first night. I did not accept of this, till I had let you know it. If you think it more convenient to carry me to your lodg-ing, make no scruple of it. Let it be what it will; if I am your wife, I shall think no place unfit for me where you are. I beg we may leave London next morning, where ever you intend to go. I should wish to go out of England if it suits with your affairs. You are the best judge of your father's temper. If you think it would be obliging to him, or necessary for you, I will go with you immediately to ask his pardon and his blessing. If that is not proper at first, I think the best scheme is going to the spa. When you come back you may endeavour to make your father admit of seeing me, and treat with mine (tho' I persist in thinking it will be to no purpose). But I cannot think of living in the midst of my relations and acquaintance after so unjustifiable a step – unjustifiable to the world. – But I think I can justify my self to my self.

I again beg you to hire a coach to be at the door early Monday morning to carry us some part of our way, wherever you resolve our journey shall be. If you determine to go to the lady's house, you had better come with a coach and six at 7 o'clock tomorrow. She and I will be in the balcony that looks on the road; you have nothing to do but to stop under it, and we will come down to you. Do in this what you like best. After all, think very seriously. Your letter which will be waited for, is to determine every thing. I forgive you a coarse expression in your last, which however I wish had not been there. You might have said something like it without expressing it in that manner, but there was so much complaisance in the rest of it, I ought to be satisfied. You can show me no goodness I shall not be sensible of. However, think again, and resolve never to think of me if you have the least doubt, or that it is likely to make you uneasy in your fortune. I believe to travel is the most likely way to make a solitude agreeable, and not tiresome. Remember you have promised it.

'Tis something odd for a woman that brings nothing to expect any thing, but after the way of my education I dare not pretend to live but in some degree suitable to it. I had rather die than return to a dependency upon relations I have disobliged. Save me from that fear if you love me. If you cannot, or think I ought not to expect it, be sincere and tell me so. 'Tis better I should not be yours at all, than for a short happiness involve my self in ages of misery. I hope there will never be occasion for this precaution but however 'tis necessary to make it. I depend entirely on your honour, and I cannot suspect you of any way doing wrong. Do not imagine I shall be angry at anything you can tell me. Let it be sincere. Do not impose on a woman that leaves all things for you.

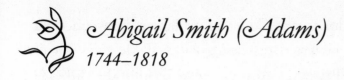

Abigail Smith (Adams)
1744–1818

Abigail Smith was born in Weymouth, Massachusetts, the daughter of William Smith, a minister, and Elizabeth Quincy, whose father was active in politics and government and was for forty years the Speaker of the Massachusetts Assembly. Abigail grew up without a formal education, but was encouraged by her father and her maternal grandfather to read widely in their extensive libraries.

She married John Adams, a Harvard lawyer, in 1764, and they settled on a farm near Adams' birthplace outside Boston while he built up his law practice in the city. It was in 1774, when John Adams went to Philadelphia to serve as the Massachusetts delegate to the First Continental Congress, that the couple embarked on a lifelong correspondence numbering more than 1,100 letters, which provides an invaluable portrait both of their marriage and the extraordinarily eventful times through which they lived.

John Adams, after serving in the Continental Congress and taking a large role in the drafting and defending of the Declaration of Independence, was posted to France and then Britain as the first US ambassador to the Court of St James; between 1778 and 1785 he was overseas a great deal. He and Abigail continued to write to each other despite the difficulties of a transatlantic correspondence; he kept her informed about the international situation, and she kept him apprised of how things stood at home, in both the governmental and the domestic spheres. Abigail joined him in 1783 and explored both Paris and London, where the couple were received by the king.

John Adams became the first vice-president of the United States in 1789, and was elected as its second president in 1797. Mr and Mrs Adams lived in the White House for only four months, from November 1800, during which time Abigail famously hung her family's laundry to dry in the unfinished East Room. She was regularly consulted by her husband on matters of policy – her influence led to her being criticized in the press and derisively referred to as 'Mrs President', a line of attack that remains wearisomely familiar. When the president was defeated for re-election by Thomas Jefferson, he and Abigail retired to Massachusetts, where they remained for the rest of their lives. Abigail died in 1818, six years before her son John Quincy Adams became the sixth president of the United States.

The letters below can give only a tiny flavour of the fascinating correspondence between this most devoted of couples. The second letter here was written as Congress was drafting the Declaration of Independence, and Abigail exhorts her husband to 'Remember the Ladies, and be more generous and favourable to them than your ancestors. Do not put such unlimited power into the hands of the Husbands. Remember all Men would be tyrants if they could.'

To John Adams
Sent from Braintree, 19 August 1774

The great distance between us, makes the time appear very long to me. It seems already a month since you left me. The great anxiety I feel for my Country, for you and for our family renders the day tedious, and the night unpleasent. The Rocks and quick Sands appear upon every Side. What course you can or will take is all wrapt in the Bosom of futurity. Uncertainty and expectation leave the mind great Scope. Did ever any Kingdom or State regain their Liberty, when once it was invaded without Blood shed? I cannot think of it without horror.

Yet we are told that all the Misfortunes of Sparta were occasiond by their too great Sollicitude for present tranquility, and by an excessive love of peace they neglected the means of making it sure and lasting. They ought to have reflected says Polibius that as there is nothing more desirable, or advantages than peace, when founded in justice and honour, so there is nothing more shameful and at the same time more pernicious when attained by bad measures, and purchased at the price of liberty. [. . .]

I have taken a very great fondness for reading Rollin's ancient History since you left me. I am determined to go thro with it if posible in these my days of solitude. I find great pleasure and entertainment from it, and I have perswaided Johnny to read me a page or two every day, and hope he will from his desire to oblige me entertain a fondness for it. – We have had a charming rain which lasted 12 hours and has greatly revived the dying fruits of the earth.

I want much to hear from you. I long impatiently to have you upon the Stage of action. The first of September or the month of September, perhaps may be of as much importance to Great Britan as the Ides of March were to Ceaser. I wish you every Publick as well, as private blessing, and that wisdom which is profitable both for instruction and edification to conduct you in this difficult day. – The little flock remember Pappa, and kindly wish to see him. So does your most affectionate

Abigail Adams

I wish you would ever write me a Letter half as long as I write you; and tell me if you may where your Fleet are gone? What sort of Defence Virginia can make against our common Enemy? Whether it is so situated as to make an able Defence? Are not the Gentery Lords and the common people vassals, are they not like the uncivilized Natives Brittain represents us to be? I hope their Riffel Men who have shewen themselves very savage and even Blood thirsty; are not a specimen of the Generality of the people.

I am willing to allow the Colony great merit for having produced a Washington but they have been shamefully duped by a Dunmore.

I have sometimes been ready to think that the passion for Liberty cannot be Eaquelly Strong in the Breasts of those who have been accustomed to deprive their fellow Creatures of theirs. Of this I am certain that it is not founded upon that generous and christian principal of doing to others as we would that others should do unto us.

Do not you want to see Boston; I am fearfull of the small pox, or I should have been in before this time. I got Mr. Crane to go to our House and see what state it was in. I find it has been occupied by one of the Doctors of a Regiment, very dirty, but no other damage has been done to it. The few things which were left in it are all gone. Cranch has the key which he never deliverd up. I have wrote to him for it and am determined to get it cleand as soon as possible and shut it up. I look upon it a new acquisition of property, a property which one month ago I did not value at a single Shilling, and could with pleasure have seen it in flames.

The Town in General is left in a better state than we expected, more oweing to a percipitate flight than any Regard to the inhabitants, tho some individuals discoverd a sense of honour and justice and have left the rent of the Houses in which they were, for the owners and the furniture unhurt, or if damaged sufficent to make it good.

Others have committed abominable Ravages. The Mansion House of your President is safe and the furniture unhurt whilst both the House and Furniture of the Solisiter General have fallen a prey to their own merciless party. Surely the very Fiends feel a Reverential awe for Virtue and patriotism, whilst they Detest the paricide and traitor.

I feel very differently at the approach of spring to what I did a month ago. We knew not then whether we could plant or sow with safety, whether when we had toild we could reap the fruits of our own industery, whether we could rest in our own Cottages, or whether we should not be driven from the sea coasts to seek shelter in the wilderness, but now we feel as if we might sit under our own vine and eat the good of the land.

I feel a gaieti de Coar to which before I was a stranger. I think the Sun looks brighter, the Birds sing more melodiously, and Nature puts on a more chearfull countanance. We feel a temporary peace, and the poor fugitives are returning to their deserted habitations.

Tho we felicitate ourselves, we sympathize with those who are trembling least the Lot of Boston should be theirs. But they cannot be in similar circumstances unless pusil-animity and cowardise should take possession of them. They have time and warning given them to see the Evil and shun it. – I long to hear that you have declared an independency – and by the way in the new Code of Laws which I suppose it will be necessary for you to make I desire you would Remember the Ladies, and be more generous and favourable to them than your ancestors. Do not put such unlimited power into the hands of the Husbands. Remember all Men would be tyrants if they could. If perticuliar care and atten-tion is not paid to the Laidies we are determined to foment a Rebelion, and will not hold ourselves bound by any Laws in which we have no voice, or Representation.

That your Sex are Naturally Tyrannical is a Truth so thoroughly established as to admit of no dispute, but such of you as wish to be happy willingly give up the harsh title of Master for the more tender and endearing one of Friend. Why then, not put it out of the power of the vicious and the Lawless to use us with cruelty and indignity with impunity. Men of Sense in all Ages abhor those customs which treat us only as the vassals of your Sex. Regard us then as Beings placed by providence under your protection and in immitation of the Supreem Being make use of that power only for our happiness.

Not having an opportunity of sending this I shall add a few lines more; tho not with a heart so gay. I have been attending the sick chamber of our Neighbour Trot whose affliction I most sensibly feel but cannot discribe, striped of two lovely children in one week. Gorge the Eldest died on wedensday and Billy the youngest on fryday, with the Canker fever, a terible disorder so much like the throat distemper, that it differs but little from it. Betsy Cranch has been very bad, but upon the recovery. Becky Peck they do not expect will live out the day. Many grown persons are now sick with it, in this street 5. It rages much in other Towns. The Mumps too are very frequent. Isaac is now confined with it. Our own little flock are yet well. My Heart trembles with anxiety for them. God preserve them.

I want to hear much oftener from you than I do. March 8 was the last date of any that I have yet had. – You inquire of whether I am making Salt peter. I have not yet attempted it, but after Soap making believe I shall make the experiment. I find as much as I can do to manufacture cloathing for my family which would else be Naked. I know of but one person in this part of the Town who has made any, that is Mr. Tertias Bass as he is calld who has got very near an hundred weight which has been found to be very good. I have heard of some others in the other parishes. Mr. Reed of Weymouth has been applied to, to go to Andover to the mills which are now at work, and has gone. I have lately seen a small Manuscrip describing the proportions for the various sorts of powder, fit for cannon, small arms and pistols. If it would be of any Service your way I will get it transcribed and send it to you. – Every one of your Friends send their Regards, and all the little ones. Your Brothers youngest child lies bad with convulsion fitts. Adieu. I need not say how much I am Your ever faithfull Friend.

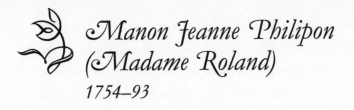

Manon Jeanne Philipon (Madame Roland)
1754–93

Marie-Jeanne Philipon (known to her friends as Manon) was the daughter of a Parisian engraver, and even as a girl demonstrated a lively and enquiring mind. She was mainly self-taught; the two biggest influences on her life were probably the writings of Plutarch and, latterly, Rousseau.

In 1781, Marie-Jeanne married Jean Roland de la Platière, a manufacturing inspector who also wrote on politics and economics and was a contributor to Diderot's Encyclopaedia. The couple moved to Lyon, where M. Roland contributed articles sympathetic to the aims of the French Revolution to the regional newspaper. In 1791 M. Roland went to Paris to appeal for help for the Lyon silk industry, which was in crisis, and became intimate with many key revolutionary figures; shortly afterwards, the couple moved there permanently, and Mme Roland became the hostess of a prominent political salon, which espoused the revolutionary cause.

With the declaration of the Republic in 1792, M. Roland was appointed interior minister, but two days after the execution of the king, he resigned his office. At this point the revolutionaries had split into two main camps, the extremist Jacobins and the more moderate Girondins amongst whom were numbered the Rolands. The Jacobins, led by Robespierre, staged a coup, which finally led to the Terror; the Girondins were summarily sentenced to death by guillotine by the Revolutionary Tribunal. Madame Roland helped her husband to flee, but she herself was arrested in June 1793 and tried on the charge of harbouring royalist sympathies. While in prison she wrote her memoirs, a document that charts the development of her intellect and her political thought and provides a fascinating history of the revolution. It also reveals Madame Roland's struggle to negotiate the path between her feelings about appropriate feminine behaviour and her gifts as a writer and intellectual.

On 8 November she was taken to the Place de la Revolution to be executed. On her way to the guillotine, she paused before the makeshift clay statue of Liberty that had been raised there and cried, 'O Liberty, what crimes are committed in thy name!' *Le Moniteur*, the revolutionary newspaper, published the following obituary: 'She was a mother, but had sacrificed nature by wishing to be above her station. The desire to be a learned woman led her to forget the virtues of her sex, and that omission, always dangerous, led her to die on the scaffold.' Her husband had escaped as far as Rouen, but on hearing of his wife's execution, he ran himself through with his sword by the side of a country road.

The letter below is to Léonard Buzot, the Rolands' fellow Girondin and possibly the lover of Madame Roland; he was on the run, but he too committed suicide in a Bordeaux forest that same year.

To Léonard Buzot
Sent from prison, 22 June 1793

How often do I not re-read your letters! I press them to my heart, I cover them with my kisses. I did not expect any more. Without success I asked for news of you from Madame Cholet. I wrote once to M. le Tellier in Evreux, so that you should receive a sign of life from me, but the postal connection is interrupted. I did not want to send you anything direct, because your name would suffice for the letter to be intercepted, and I might besides attract suspicion to you. Proud and calm I came here, with wishes for the defenders of liberty and some hopes for them. When I heard of the decree of arrest that had been promulgated against the twenty-two, I exclaimed 'My country is lost.' I remained in painful anxiety, before I had certain news of your flight, and the decree issued for your arrest frightens me anew. This horrible thing is no doubt due to your courage; since I know that you are in the Calvados, I regain my equanimity. Continue in your noble endeavours, my friend. Brutus despaired too soon of the Roman safety at the battle of Philippi. As long as a republican still breathes, is free, has his courage, he must, he can be useful. The south of France offers you in any case a refuge, and will be the asylum of honourable men. Thither you must turn your looks and wend your steps. There you will have to live, in order to serve your fellows and to exercise your virtues.

I personally shall know how to wait quietly, until the reign of justice returns, or shall undergo the last acts of violence, of tyranny in such a manner, that my example too will not be without utility . . .

Maria Smythe
(Mrs Fitzherbert)
1756–1837

Maria Anne Fitzherbert grew up in Hampshire, the daughter of a Walter Smythe, a former soldier, and his wife Mary Errington; both families were Catholic. At about twelve, she was sent to a Parisian convent for her education. She married and was widowed twice by 1781, leaving her a young woman of independent means.

The Prince of Wales, who was to become Prince Regent and eventually George IV, began his pursuit of her in 1784 after a chance meeting outside the opera house. She refused to become his mistress, and he eventually begged her to marry him, notwithstanding the three Acts of Parliament that stood in their way (the Act of Settlement, the Act of Union and the Royal Marriages Act). Mrs Fitzherbert declined his proposal and announced her intention to travel abroad. As a result the not notably restrained prince stabbed himself at his London home, Carlton House in Pall Mall, and dispatched his surgeon and three other friends to tell her that he would tear off his bandages unless she came immediately. She did, in company with Georgiana, Duchess of Devonshire, and the hysterical prince extracted from her a promise to marry him. She then left the country for Europe.

While she was away, the prince inundated her with letters, and although Mrs Fitzherbert regarded a promise made under such duress to be void, she eventually relented and agreed to marry him. The prince arranged the secret wedding, and in early November 1785 wrote her an impassioned forty-two-page letter; she returned to London the following month, and they were married in the drawing room of her house in Park Street on 15 December.

The prince then installed Mrs Fitzherbert in a house near his own in Pall Mall, but she was constantly exposed to insults and ridicule; speculation about the pair was feverish among their circle, in the press and in Parliament. There were (unfounded) hints that she was involved in a Catholic plot to destabilize the government. Another problem was the prince himself; he had managed to amass quite surreal debts as he turned Carlton House into a kind of fantasy palace, employing craftsmen from all over Europe, importing furniture from China and knocking down adjoining houses to make way for new wings. At one point, his treasurer, asked to calculate the money owed, professed it 'beyond all calculation whatever'. And, furthermore, he could not keep away from the ladies, despite the lengths to which he had gone to marry Mrs Fitzherbert. Eventually, the disapproving George III insisted that a suitable royal bride must be found for his wayward son, and the prince was more or less forced to marry Princess Caroline of Brunswick. In April 1795, exactly nine months after the wedding, Caroline gave birth to their only child, Princess Charlotte; by then, the couple were already living apart.

The prince and Mrs Fitzherbert were separated and reconciled several times up until 1811, when the rift became permanent; after this, the pair saw very little of each other. The prince's life became increasingly dissolute and scandalous; he was a gift to the caricaturists – immensely fat, painted and preening, drunk and gluttonous. Mrs Fitzherbert did write to him during his final illness in 1830; he was too ill to reply, but he died with a miniature of her around his neck, which was placed in his coffin. She died seven years later, at home in Brighton, discreet to the end.

To the Prince Regent

I was drawn to the Steine [a fashionable promenading area of Brighton] this evening by a party who drank tea with us and would not excuse me (though I was really too ill to go out) because it was generally believed that your —— —— [Royal Highness], in imitation of a ridiculous Frenchman, was to run a race backwards! Oh, that you had a mentor to guard you from those numerous perils that around you wait! The greatest of which are your present companions. As I beheld you the other day like another Harry:

> *Rise from the ground like feathered Mercury,*
> *and vaulted with such ease into your seat*
> *as if an angel dropt down from the clouds;*
> *to turn and wind a fiery Pegasus,*
> *and witch the world with noble horsemanship . . .*

I could not avoid continuing the comparison, and wish that you would sometimes use that Prince's words:

> *Reply not to me with a fool-born jest,*
> *for Heaven doth know, so shall the world perceive;*
> *That I have turned away from my former self,*
> *so will I those that kept me company.*

Adieu! If I am free to remember it is your own condescension that draws on you the remarks of

Margarita

To the Prince Regent

You will compel me to leave B*******, I am offended at your behaviour of last night. Why did I seek a walk retired? had we met on the Steine you would have been more guarded; alas! you have not the delicacy I wished! When you talk of love you offer an insult you are insensible of – your friendship confers honour; but your love – retain it for some worthy fair, born to the high honour of becoming your wife, and repine not that fate has placed my lot – in humble life. I am content with my station: content has charms that are not to be expressed. I know I am wrong in continuing this correspondence; – it must – it ought to cease: write therefore no more to

Margarita

Mary Wollstonecraft
1759–97

Mary Wollstonecraft was born to a fairly well-to-do family in Spitalfields, east London, the second of seven children. Her father was, by her account, an alcoholic and a bully. Mary received scant formal education; her impressive learning was the result of her own self-discipline and determination.

By the time she reached adulthood, the family's means had dwindled to nothing, and Mary needed to earn a living. She worked unhappily as a teacher, a governess and a lady's companion before she took up writing, and in 1787 she published her first book, *Thoughts on the Education of Daughters*. Her publisher, Joseph Johnson, employed her to write essays for his magazine, the *Analytical Review*; he also became a lifelong friend and mentor, and presumably a far more satisfactory paternal presence than her father had ever been.

Throughout the 1780s, Wollstonecraft lived the unremarkable life of a literary hack, although her appearance did raise some eyebrows: rough garments, worsted black stockings, unkempt hair which she refused to pin up. This early attempt to forge an identity which she felt was true to herself, rather than feminine convention (a precursor perhaps of the dungaree phase of twentieth-century feminism), was the beginning of a struggle which lasted her whole life.

Wollstonecraft's first big success came with her publication in 1790 of *A Vindication of the Rights of Men*, a riposte to Edmund Burke's post-revolutionary apologia for France's Ancien Régime. Mary was fêted as a leading radical, but she soon became frustrated with the lack of progress towards equal rights for women in this supposedly enlightened new age. She was inspired to write, in three months, her most celebrated work, *A Vindication of the Rights of Women*, which was published in 1792 and became an immediate international bestseller.

That same year, after an unhappy love affair with a married bisexual painter named Henry Fuseli (at one point, Mary had approached Fuseli's wife Sophia to propose a *ménage à trois* in which Mary would be recognized as Fuseli's 'spiritual spouse' – whatever that might have meant; a furious Sophia threw her out), Wollstonecraft travelled to Paris, where she met Captain Gilbert Imlay, an American soldier turned entrepreneur – handsome, charming and (inevitably) a well-known womanizer. By the end of 1793, Mary was pregnant, but after registering her as his wife at the

American embassy, Imlay disappeared on business. Abandoned and anxious, she followed him first to Le Havre, where her daughter Fanny was born in May 1794, and then to London, hoping to establish some kind of family life. Imlay did not share this ambition and was routinely unfaithful; the relationship dragged on until 1796. During that time she attempted suicide twice, once by swallowing a lethal dose of opium (she was rescued by a servant) and once by throwing herself into the Thames by Putney Bridge (she was pulled out by two passing boatmen).

After the final break from Imlay, Mary published *A Short Residence in Sweden, Norway and Denmark*, which she had written when she had travelled through Scandinavia, at Imlay's behest, in order to sort out some business affairs of his there. It was then she had realized there was no future to be had with Imlay, and this book, part memoir, part travelogue, part polemic, is her most personal.

Mary had first met William Godwin, the radical writer, in 1791, but it wasn't until 1796, when she took the bold (for the time) step of calling on him, ostensibly to lend him a book, that they fell deeply in love. By early 1797 Mary was pregnant and, despite the hostility both parties had expressed towards the institution of matrimony, they were married that March.

Their daughter, Mary Wollstonecraft Godwin, later Mary Shelley, was born on 30 August. Mary Wollstonecraft died of puerperal fever eleven days later. Her devastated husband wrote to a friend, 'I have not the least expectation that I can now ever know happiness again.'

In 1801, William Godwin married a neighbour, Mary Jane Vial, the mother of Claire Clairmont, whose letter to Byron appears elsewhere in this collection.

To Gilbert Imlay
Sent from Paris, Friday morning, 1793

I am glad to find that other people can be unreasonable as well as myself; for be it known to thee that I answered thy *first* letter the very night it reached me (Sunday), though thou couldst not receive it before Wednesday, because it was not sent off till the next day. There is a full, true, and particular account.

Yet I am not angry with thee, my love, for I think that it is a proof of stupidity, and likewise of a milk-and-water affection, which comes to the same thing when the temper is governed by a square and compass. There is nothing picturesque in the straight-lined equality, and the passions always give grace to the actions.

Recollection now makes my heart bound to thee; but it is

not to thy money-getting face, though I cannot be seriously displeased with the exertion which increases my esteem, or rather it is what I should have expected from thy character. No; I have thy honest countenance before me – relaxed by tenderness; a little – little wounded by my whims; and thy eyes glittering with sympathy. Thy lips then feel softer than soft, and I rest my cheek on thine, forgetting all the world. I have not left the hue of love out of the picture – the rosy glow; and fancy has spread it over my own cheeks, I believe, for I feel them burning, whilst a delicious tear trembles in my eye that would be all your own, if a grateful emotion directed to the Father of nature, who has made me thus alive to happiness, did not give more warmth to the sentiment it divides. I must pause a moment.

Need I tell you that I am tranquil after writing thus? I do not know why, but I have more confidence in your affection, when absent, than present; nay, I think that you must love me, for, in the sincerity of my heart let me say it, I believe I deserve your tenderness, because I am true, and have a degree of sensibility that you can see and relish.

Yours sincerely,

Mary

To Gilbert Imlay
Sent from Paris, evening, 23 September 1794

I have been playing and laughing with the little girl so long, that I cannot take up my pen to address you without emotion. Pressing her to my bosom, she looked so like you (entre nous, your best looks, for I do not admire your commercial face), every nerve seemed to vibrate to the touch, and I began to think that there was something in the assertion of man and wife being one – for you seemed to pervade my whole frame, quickening the beat of my heart, and lending me the sympathetic tears you excited.

Have I anything more to say to you? No; not for the present – the rest is all flown away; and indulging tenderness for you, I cannot now complain of some people here, who have ruffled my temper for two or three days past.

To William Godwin, 21 July 1796

I send you, as requested, the altered m.s. Had you called upon me yesterday I should have thanked you for your letter – and – perhaps, have told you that the sentence I *liked* best was the concluding one, where you tell me, that you were coming home, to depart *no more* – But now I am out of humour I mean to bottle up my kindness, unless something in your countenance, when I do see you, should make the cork fly out – whether I will or not –

Mary

Thursday

Judd Place West

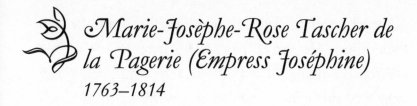

Marie-Josèphe-Rose Tascher de la Pagerie (Empress Joséphine)
1763–1814

Joséphine, as she was always called by Napoleon, was born in Martinique, the daughter of a wealthy plantation-owning family whose estates were destroyed by hurricanes in 1766. She left for Paris in 1779 to make an advantageous marriage to Alexandre, vicomte de Beauharnais, a French aristocrat. The marriage was not happy, although Joséphine bore him two children, Hortense and Eugène, before obtaining a legal separation in 1785. In 1788, she returned to Martinique, but left again for Paris in 1790 after a slave uprising on the island.

Joséphine led a glittering social life in Paris and maintained liaisons with several prominent men, but her life was endangered when her husband fell foul of the revolutionary Jacobins and was guillotined in June 1794. She was imprisoned, but was released after Robespierre himself was executed the following month. It was after her release and the establishment of the government of the Directory that she met Napoleon Bonaparte, a brilliant young army officer.

They were married in March 1796, just before

Napoleon left for Italy as commander of the French expedition. He wrote passionate love letters to her constantly, many of which survive, while there are very few surviving letters from Joséphine to her husband; either they were destroyed or they never existed. The latter explanation, it has to be said, seems the more likely one, as Joséphine was apparently a less than devoted wife, of dubious fidelity and tastes that ran from the merely expensive to the straightforwardly ruinous. Napoleon often complained bitterly both of her flirtations with other men and of her extravagance, and in 1799 threatened to divorce her; he was eventually persuaded against it by the intercession of her children by her first husband.

Napoleon's military and political success appeared unstoppable, and he was crowned Emperor of France in 1804 by Pope Pius VII (legend has it that he seized the crown from the Pope's hands at the moment of coronation and put it on his own head). He then crowned Joséphine Empress.

Joséphine's future now appeared secure: she was Empress of France, with her son married to the daughter of the king of Bavaria, and her daughter to Napoleon's brother. But her own marriage continued under strain, and in 1810 Napoleon was granted an annulment. Now he was Emperor he needed an heir, and with Joséphine unable to provide one he had set his sights on a dynastic marriage with the daughter of the Emperor of Austria.

Joséphine withdrew to the Château de Malmaison outside Paris, where she appears to have lived quite happily, entertaining her friends and protectors (who included Tsar Nicholas I) while remaining on good terms with Napoleon, who continued to pay her bills. The letter below dates from that time. She died of pneumonia four years later, and is buried in the nearby parish church of Reuil. The royal families of Holland, Luxembourg, Sweden, Belgium, Greece and Denmark are all descended from her. Napoleon's last words, when he died in exile on St Helena in 1821, were reported to be, 'France, the army, Joséphine.'

To Napoleon Bonaparte
Sent from Navarra, April 1810

A thousand, thousand tender thanks for not having forgotten me. My son has just brought me your letter. With what ardour I read it and yet I spent much time on it; for there was not a word in it that did not make me weep. But those tears were so sweet. I found again my whole heart, and such as it will always be; there are sentiments which are life itself, and which can only finish with it.

I would be in despair if my letter of the 19th had displeased you; I do not entirely remember its expressions, but I know what very painful sentiment had dictated it, it was the chagrin not to have had news from you.

I had written you at my departure from Malmaison; and since then, how many times did I not wish to write to you! But I felt the reason of your silence, and I feared to be importunate by a letter. Yours has been a balm for me. Be happy; be it as much as you deserve it; it is my entire heart that speaks to you. You also have just given me my share of happiness, and a share very vividly felt; nothing can equal the value for me of a mark of your remembrance.

Adieu, my friend; I thank you as tenderly as I shall always love you.

Joséphine

Mary Hutchinson (Wordsworth)
1782–1859

Mary Hutchinson married the great Romantic poet William Wordsworth in 1802; she was an old school friend of Wordsworth's sister, Dorothy, who until the marriage had been Wordsworth's principal companion. Dorothy recorded the wedding day in her journal:

On Monday 4 October 1802, my brother William was married to Mary Hutchinson. I slept a good deal of the night and rose fresh and well in the morning. At a little after 8 o'clock I saw them go down the avenue towards the Church. William had parted from me upstairs. I gave him the wedding ring – with how deep a blessing! I took it from my forefinger where I had worn it the whole of the night before – he slipped it again onto my finger and blessed me fervently. When they were absent my dear little Sara [Hutchinson, sister of the bride] prepared the breakfast. I kept myself as quiet as I could, but when I saw the two men running up the walk, coming to tell us it was over, I could stand it no longer and threw myself on the bed where I lay in stillness, neither hearing or seeing anything, till Sara came upstairs to me and said, 'They are coming.' This forced me from the bed where I lay and I moved I knew not how straight

forward, faster than my strength could carry me till I
met my beloved William and fell upon his bosom. He
and John Hutchinson led me to the house and there
I stayed to welcome my dear Mary.

So: on her wedding day, Mary Wordsworth had to
look on with forbearance while her husband's sister
managed to work herself up into a hysterical fit in
which she was 'neither hearing or seeing anything',
and then, in welcoming Mary to her new home,
ensured that it was she who accompanied her brother
over the threshold, rather than his bride.

Wordsworth's relationship with his sister and its
influence on his work has been written about exten-
sively; his relationship with his wife was barely even
acknowledged until a cache of letters between
Wordsworth and Mary were auctioned at Sotheby's in
1977. The letters revealed a marriage full of passion
and affection, which is absolutely remarkable consid-
ering the circumstances of their domestic life. They
were short of money; they shared their house with
Dorothy and with Mary's sister, Sara, as well as an
assortment of poets and critics including the increasingly drug-dependent nuisance that was Coleridge;
and between 1803 and 1810, Mary gave birth to five
children, two of whom died in 1812 plunging her into

a deep depression. Later on life became slightly easier, as Wordsworth became more successful (he was appointed poet laureate in 1845), and the household moved to more spacious accommodation which afforded everyone more privacy, but the fact that the arrangements seem to have worked at all must be a testament to Mary's extraordinary patience.

In 1835, Dorothy was struck with some kind of pre-senile dementia; she was nursed by Mary for the last twenty years of her life. Wordsworth died in 1850; Mary outlived them both, dying in 1859. All three are buried in the churchyard at St Oswald's, Grasmere, in the Lake District, the landscape of which had provided Wordsworth with lifelong inspiration.

To William Wordsworth
Sent from Grasmere, Monday 1 August to Wednesday morning 3 August c.1810

O My William!
It is not in my power to tell thee how I have been affected by this dearest of all letters – it was so unexpected – so new a thing to see the breathing of thy inmost heart upon paper that I was quite overpowered, & now that I sit down to answer thee in the loneliness & depth of that love which unites us & which cannot be felt but by ourselves, I am so

agitated & my eyes are so bedimmed that I scarcely know how to proceed – I have brought my paper, after having laid my baby upon thy sacred pillow, into my own, into THY own room – & write from Sara's little Table, retired from the window which looks upon the lasses strewing out the hay to an uncertain Sun. – [. . .]

I look upon thy letter & I marvel how thou hast managed to write it so legibly, for there is not a word in it, that I could have a doubt about. But how is it that I have not received it sooner – It was written on *Sunday* before last – last Sunday *Morning* I rec^d. One of Dear Dorothy's written on the *Monday* & another in the evening of the same day, written on the *Thursday*; both *since* that day when my good angel put it into thy thoughts to make me so happy – Dorothy has asked me more than once when she has found me this morning with thy letter in my hand 'what I was crying about' – I told her that I was *so happy* – but she could not comprehend this. Indeed my love it has made me supremely blessed – it has given me a new feeling, for it is the first letter of love that has been exclusively my own – Wonder not then that I have been so affected by it.

Dearest William! I am sorry about thy eye – that it is not well before now, & I am SORRY for what causes in me such pious & exulting gladness – that you cannot fully enjoy your absence from me – indeed William I feel, I *have felt* that you cannot, but it overpowers me to be told it by your own pen *I* was much moved by the lines written with your hand in one of D's letters where you spoke of coming home thinking you 'would be of great use' to me – indeed my love thou wouldst but I did not *want thee* so much *then*, as I do now that our uncomfortableness is passed away – if you had been here, no *doubt* there would have existed in me that underconsciousness that I had my *all in all* about me – *that* feeling which I have never wanted since* the solitary night did not separate us, except in absence; but I had not then that leisure which I ought to have & which is necessary to be actively alive to so rich a possession & to the full enjoyment of it – I *do* William & I shall to the end of my life consider this sacrifice as a dear offering of thy love, I feel it to be such, & I am grateful to thee for it but I trust that it will be the last of the kind that we shall need to make –

* 'I slept with' was deleted

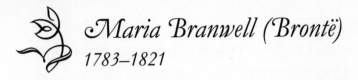

Maria Branwell (Brontë)
1783–1821

The mother of the great novelists Charlotte, Emily and Anne was born in Penzance, Cornwall, the eighth of eleven children. Her parents, Thomas Branwell and Anne Carne, were both from prosperous families, and were leading members of the Wesleyan Methodist community.

Both Maria's parents died when she was in her twenties. Her aunt, her father's sister Jane, invited Maria to join her at Rawdon near Leeds, where her husband, John Fennell, was the headmaster of a school, and in 1812 Maria left Penzance for a new life in Yorkshire.

Patrick Brontë, an old friend of John Fennell's, was the curate in a nearby parish, who met Maria when he visited Fennell's new school. The dates on the letters here demonstrate that the courtship between the two was short and intense; Patrick would regularly walk a round trip of twenty-four miles in order to take Maria for – a walk. By the end of the year, they were married.

Maria gave birth to six children between 1814 and 1820, the year the family moved to the famous parsonage at Howarth. The following year, after months of suffering, Maria died; the cause of death is now thought to have been chronic pelvic sepsis brought on by rapid childbearing, combined with anaemia. Four years later, her two elder daughters, Maria and Elizabeth, died of pulmonary tuberculosis contracted at the boarding school immortalized as Lowood by Charlotte in her fiction. By 1855, all the children had died, Charlotte and Emily having completed two of the greatest novels in the English language, *Jane Eyre* and *Wuthering Heights*. Patrick outlived them all, dying in 1861.

To Rev. Patrick Brontë, A.B., Hartshead
Sent from Wood House Grove, 26 August 1812

My dear Friend, This address is sufficient to convince you that I not only permit, but approve of yours to me – I do indeed consider you as my *friend*; yet when I consider how short a time I have had the pleasure of knowing you, I start at my own rashness, my heart fails, and did I not think that you would be disappointed and grieved, I believe I should be ready to spare myself the task of writing. Do not think I am so wavering as to repent of what I have already said. No, believe me, this will never be the case, unless you give me cause for it.

You need not fear that you have been mistaken in my

character. If I know anything of myself, I am incapable of making an ungenerous return to the smallest degree of kindness, much less to you whose attentions and conduct have been so particularly obliging. I will frankly confess that your behaviour and what I have seen and heard of your character has excited my warmest esteem and regard, and be assured you shall never have cause to repent of any confidence you may think proper to place in me, and that it will always be my endeavour to deserve the good opinion which you have formed, although human weakness may in some instances cause me to fall short. In giving you these assurances I do not depend upon my own strength, but I look to Him who has been my unerring guide through life, and in whose continued protection and assistance I confidently trust.

I thought on you much on Sunday, and feared you would not escape the rain. I hope you do not feel any bad effects from it? My cousin wrote you on Monday and expects this afternoon to be favoured with an answer. Your letter has caused me some foolish embarrassment, tho' in pity to my feelings they have been very sparing of their raillery.

I will now candidly answer your questions. The *politeness of others* can never make me forget your kind attentions, neither can *I walk our accustomed rounds* without thinking on you, and, why should I be ashamed to add, wishing for your presence. If you knew what were my feelings whilst writing this you would pity me. I wish to write the truth and give you satisfaction, yet fear to go too far, and exceed the bounds of propriety. But whatever I may say or write I will *never deceive* you, or *exceed the truth*. If you think I have not placed the *utmost confidence* in you, consider my situation, and ask yourself if I have not confided in you sufficiently, perhaps too much. I am very sorry that you will not have this till after tomorrow, but it was out of my power to write sooner. I rely on your goodness to pardon everything in this which may appear either too free or too stiff, and beg that you will consider me as a warm and faithful friend.

My uncle, aunt, and cousin unite in kind regards.

I must now conclude with again declaring myself to be Yours sincerely, Maria Branwell

To Rev. Patrick Brontë, A.B., Hartshead, 3 October 1812

How could my dear friend so cruelly disappoint me? Had he known how much I had set my heart on having a letter this afternoon, and how greatly I felt the disappointment when the bag arrived and I found there was nothing for me, I am sure he would not have permitted a little matter to hinder him. But whatever was the reason of your not writing, I cannot believe it to have been neglect or unkindness, therefore I do not in the least blame you, I only beg that in future you will judge of my feelings by your own, and if possible never let me expect a letter without receiving one . . . May I hope that there is now some intelligence on the way to me? or must my patience be tried till I see you on Wednesday? But what nonsense am I writing! Surely after this you can have no doubt that you possess all my heart. Two months ago I could not possibly have believed that you would ever engross so much of my thoughts and affections, and far less could I have thought that I should be so forward as to tell you so. I believe I must forbid you to come here again unless you can assure me that you will not steal any more of my regard . . .

I must now take my leave. I believe I need scarcely assure you that I am yours truly and very affectionately,

Maria Branwell

To Rev. Patrick Brontë, A.B., Hartshead, 21 October 1812

With the sincerest pleasure do I retire from company to converse with him whom I love beyond all others. Could my beloved friend see my heart he would then be convinced that the affection I bear him is not at all inferior to that which he feels for me – indeed I sometimes think that in truth and constancy it excels. But do not think from this that I entertain any suspicions of your sincerity – no, I firmly believe you to be sincere and generous, and doubt not in the least that you feel all you express. In return, I entreat that you will do me the justice to believe that you have not only a *very large portion* of my *affection* and *esteem*, but *all* that I am capable of feeling, and from henceforth measure my feelings by your own. Unless my love for you were very great how could I so contentedly give up my home and all my friends – a home I loved so much that I have often thought nothing could bribe me to renounce it for any great length of time together, and friends with whom I have been so long accustomed to share all the vicissitudes of joy and sorrow? Yet these have lost their weight, and though I cannot always think of them without a sigh, yet the anticipation of sharing with you all the pleasures and pains, the cares and anxieties of life, of contributing to your comfort and becoming the companion of your pilgrimage, is more delightful to me than any other prospect which this world can possibly present . . .

I should have been very glad to have had it in my power to lessen your fatigue and cheer your spirits by my exertions on Monday last. I will hope that this pleasure is still reserved for me. In general, I feel a calm confidence in the providential care and continued mercy of God, and when I consider His past deliverances and past favours I am led to wonder and adore. A sense of my small returns of love and gratitude to Him often abases me and makes me think I am little better than those who profess no religion. Pray for me, my dear friend, and rest assured that you possess a very, very large portion of the prayers, thoughts and heart of yours truly,

M. Branwell

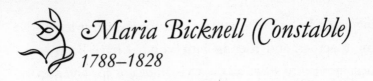

Maria Bicknell (Constable)
1788–1828

Maria Bicknell met John Constable for the first time in 1800, when as a twelve-year-old child she came to East Bergholt in the Stour Valley to visit her grandfather, Durand Rhudde, the wealthy rector there. It wasn't until 1809 that Maria and Constable fell in love, but Durand Rhudde objected vehemently to the match, and threatened to disinherit not only his granddaughter, but her four siblings as well if it were allowed to proceed.

John Constable had lived in East Bergholt all his life, where his father was a merchant and mill owner. He loved painting and drawing from an early age, and escaped from the family business as soon as he could in order to pursue his artistic studies. In 1809, he was still a struggling young artist, committed to his vision of landscape painting (rather than the more lucrative portraiture), beginning to make some progress but still subsidized by family and friends.

For the next seven years, Maria and Constable managed their courtship through clandestine meetings and a secret correspondence, while Constable persevered with his artistic career. By 1816, despite Dr Rhudde's still implacable objection, Maria was persuaded that enough was enough, and the couple were married that October. (Dr Rhudde eventually softened sufficiently to bequeath her the same portion as her siblings when he died in 1819.) Despite Constable's dislike of portraiture, in July 1816, just after Maria had agreed finally to marry him, he executed a very touching likeness of her (now in the Tate collection), of which he wrote to her, 'I am sitting before your portrait – which when I look off the paper – is so extremely like that I can hardly help going up to it – I never had an idea before of the real pleasure that a portrait could afford.'

The obstacle to happiness in his personal life overcome, Constable's struggle to have his style of landscape painting accepted by the Academy, the critics and the public continued for decades. Maria's health was fragile, and she died of consumption in 1828, having given birth to seven children in eleven years. Constable was finally elected to full membership of the Academy three months later. He died in 1837; his paintings, many of which he refused to sell during his lifetime, now change hands for vast sums, and hang in galleries all over the world. His merits are still the subject of hot dispute.

My dear Sir, – I have just received my father's letter. It is precisely such a one as I expected, reasonable and kind; his only objection would be on the score of that necessary evil money. What can we do? I wish I had it, but wishes are vain: we must be wise, and leave off a correspondence that is not calculated to make us think less of each other. We have many painful trials required of us in this life, and we must learn to bear them with resignation. You will still be my friend, and I will be yours; then as such let me advise you to go into Suffolk, you cannot fail to be better there. I have written to papa, though I do not in conscience think that he can retract anything he has said, if so, I had better not write to you any more, at least till I can coin. We should both of us be bad subjects for poverty, should we not? Even painting would go on badly, it could hardly survive in domestic worry.

By a sedulous attention to your profession you will very much help to bestow calm on my mind . . . you will allow others to outstrip you, and then perhaps blame me. Exert yourself while it is yet in your power, the path of duty is alone the path of happiness . . . Believe me, I shall feel a more lasting pleasure in knowing that you are improving your time, than I should do while you were on a stolen march with me round the Park. Still I am not heroine enough to say, wish or mean that we should never meet. I know that to be impossible. But then, let us resolve it shall be but seldom; not as inclination, but as prudence shall dictate. Farewell, dearest John – may every blessing attend you, and in the interest I feel in your welfare, forgive the advice I have given you, who, I am sure, are better qualified to admonish me. Resolution is, I think, what we now stand most in need of, to refrain for a time, for our mutual good, from the society of each other.

To John Constable, 15 September 1816

Papa is averse to everything I propose. If you please you may write to him; it will do neither good nor harm. I hope we are not going to do a very foolish thing . . . Once more, and for the last time! it is not too late to follow Papa's advice, and *wait*. Notwithstanding all I have been writing, whatever you deem best I do . . . This enchanting weather gives me spirits.

Claire Clairmont
1798–1879

Claire Clairmont grew up in a tangled household. Her mother, Mary Jane Vial, called herself Mrs Clairmont, although there is no evidence of her having been married; it is likely that Claire was illegitimate. Mary Jane was an enterprising woman who worked as a French translator and editor of children's books. A neighbour of the writer and political philosopher William Godwin, she became his second wife after the death in childbirth of his first, Mary Wollstonecraft. The household in north London contained five children, none of whom had two parents in common: Claire and her half-brother Charles; her stepsister Mary Godwin; Fanny Imlay, the daughter of Mary Wollstonecraft and Gilbert Imlay; and, from 1803, William Godwin, the son of Mary Jane and William.

In 1814 Mary Godwin, Claire's stepsister, eloped to Europe with Percy Bysshe Shelley, who was himself escaping from complicated and painful entanglements including a failed marriage. They were accompanied by Claire – an uneasy arrangement, one might think, and indeed for the rest of her life, Mary Shelley, as she became, was intermittently tormented by her husband's relationship with her stepsister. On her return to London, in 1816, Claire laid siege to the poet Byron, the celebrated author of *Childe Harold*, and the infamous womanizer and ne'er-do-well whose irresistible charisma and reckless behaviour terrified anxious mamas all over London. Claire appears to have had a plan, and that summer she contrived to engineer a meeting between Mary and Percy Shelley, Byron and herself at Lake Geneva. It was during this Geneva sojourn that the new friends spent an evening telling ghost stories, and Mary Shelley began *Frankenstein*.

In January 1817, back in England, Claire gave birth to Byron's daughter Allegra. Byron had by this time tired of Claire, but wished to maintain a relationship with his daughter, and in the summer of 1818 Claire allowed Allegra to be taken to him in Venice, after which Byron discouraged further contact between the child and her mother. After a complicated series of events – the usual Byronic cocktail of sex, scandal, domestic upheaval, political intrigue and boredom – Byron placed Allegra in a convent in Bagnacavallo, against Claire's wishes. Allegra died there, possibly of typhoid, at the age of four.

For the rest of her life, Claire Clairmont supported herself by travelling all over Europe as a governess and companion, much loved by her charges and her employers, despite having to conceal from them the radical connections of her past. She died peacefully in Florence at the age of eighty-nine, and is buried there; placed in her coffin was a shawl that had belonged to Shelley. Her bitterness towards Byron remained unmitigated.

To Lord Byron, *1816*

You bid me write short to you and I have much to say. You also bade me believe that it was a fancy which made me cherish an attachment for you. It cannot be a fancy since you have been for the last year the object upon which every solitary moment led me to muse.

I do not expect you to love me, I am not worthy of your love. I feel you are superior, yet much to my surprise, more to my happiness, you betrayed passions I had believed no longer alive in your bosom. Shall I also have to ruefully experience the want of happiness? Shall I reject it when it is offered? I may appear to you imprudent, vicious; my opinions detestable, my theory depraved; but one thing, at least, time shall show you that I love gently and with affection, that I am incapable of anything approaching to the feeling of revenge or malice; I do assure you, your future will be mine, and everything you shall do or say, I shall not question.

Have you then any objection to the following plan? On

Thursday Evening we may go out of town together by some stage or mail about the distance of ten or twelve miles. There we shall be free and unknown; we can return early the following morning. I have arranged every thing here so that the slightest suspicion may not be excited. Pray do so with your people.

Will you admit me for two moments to settle with you there? Indeed I will not stay an instant after you tell me to go. Only so much may be said and done in a short time by an interview which writing cannot effect. Do what you will, or go where you will, refuse to see me and behave unkindly, I shall never forget you. I shall ever remember the gentleness of your manners and the wild originality of your countenance. Having been once seen, you are not to be forgotten. Perhaps this is the last time I shall ever address you. Once more, then, let me assure you that I am not ungrateful. In all things have you acted most honourably, and I am only provoked that the awkwardness of my manner and something like timidity has hitherto prevented my expressing it to you personally.

Clara Clairmont

Will you admit me now as I wait in Hamilton Place for your answer?

Jane Welsh (Carlyle)
1801–66

Jane Welsh was born in Haddington near Edinburgh in Scotland, an only child; her father was a doctor. Both her parents were Scottish. She was a precocious child with a lively, inquiring mind, and her father, whom she idolized, arranged for her to receive private tuition from the clergyman and scholar Edward Irving. When her father died in 1819, Jane was bereft. She had no occupation other than the fulfilment of social engagements and the manipulation of various suitors, including her former tutor, who unsuccessfully tried to break off his engagement to another woman in order to marry her. It was he who introduced her to the scholar and essayist Thomas Carlyle in 1821.

Carlyle was not considered a suitable match by Jane's mother, nor, incidentally, by Jane herself, but she valued his mind and his intellectual guidance. They were finally married in 1826. It seems that Jane saw her choice in fairly stark terms: she married Carlyle, who she regarded as a genius, in order to escape the stultifying life that otherwise awaited her in Haddington.

The Carlyles' marriage was tempestuous (the novelist Samuel Butler observed that it was 'very good of God to let Carlyle and Mrs Carlyle marry one another, and so make only two people miserable instead of four') and, while it lasted forty years, it is not even certain that it was ever consummated. Jane was an indispensable aid to her husband in his work, particularly when the almost completed manuscript of his history of the French Revolution was somehow put on the fire by the servant of a friend who had been reading it. Carlyle, with the steadfast encouragement of Jane, managed to reconstruct the whole thing.

For some time the Carlyles lived in Scotland, where Jane was lonely, isolated and miserable. It was when they moved to London in 1834 that she came into her own as a hostess, entertaining some of the most renowned writers, artists and politicians of the day, including Dickens, Thackeray and Tennyson. Her marriage encountered serious difficulty in 1843, when Thomas became infatuated with Lady Harriet Baring, who with her husband entertained in the grand style at their large house on Piccadilly or at their estate in the country. Jane, whose health was poor, drugged herself with morphine and struggled to understand how her gamble in marrying Carlyle had gone so badly wrong; she was now excluded from the circle in which she had shone, as Lady Harriet made it clear her invitations were extended to Thomas alone.

Lady Harriet died in 1857, and the final phase of the marriage was apparently happier and more tranquil than the rancour and resentment of the preceding decades. Jane Carlyle died in her carriage as she was being driven through Hyde Park in 1866. Her husband at once set to work on his *Reminiscences* and on a collection of her letters, with the avowed intention of winning for her the posthumous fame he felt she deserved. While his (possibly naive) frankness caused some scandal, his objective was largely achieved; her brilliance as a correspondent is widely recognized, and Jane Carlyle is routinely referred to as the best letter-writer in the English language. It is impossible to say whether or not, in a different time, she might have achieved success as an artist in her own right, but given her obvious talents, it is difficult not to speculate.

To Thomas Carlyle
Sent from Templand, Tuesday, 3 October 1826

Unkind that you are ever to suffer me to be cast down, when it is so easy a thing for you to lift me to the Seventh Heaven! my soul was darker than midnight when your pen said 'Let there be light,' and there *was* light at the bidding of the Word. And now I am resolved in spirit and even joyful, joyful even in the face of the dreaded ceremony, of *starvation*, and every possible fate.

Oh, my dearest Friend! be always *so* good to me, and I shall make the best and happiest Wife. When I read in your looks and words that you love me, I feel it in the deepest part of my soul; then I care not one jot for the whole Universe beside; but when you fly from my caresses to – smoke tobacco, or speak of me as a new *circumstance* of your lot, then indeed my 'heart is troubled about many things.'

My Mother is not come yet, but is expected this week; the week following must be given to her to take a last look at her Child; and then Dearest, God willing, I am your own for ever and ever . . .

Oh mercy! What I would give to be sitting in our doll's house married for a week! . . .

I may well return *one* out of *twenty*. But indeed, Dear, these kisses on paper are scarce worth keeping. You gave me one on my neck that night you were in such good-humour, and one on my lips on some forgotten occasion, that I would not part with for a hundred thousand paper ones. Perhaps some day or other, I shall get none of either sort; *sic transit gloria mundi* . . . And then not my will be done, but thine. I am going to be really a very meek-tempered Wife; indeed, I am begun to be meek-tempered already. My Aunt tells me, she could live for ever with *me*, without quarrelling – I am so reasonable and equal in my humour. There is something to gladden your heart withal! and more than this; my Grandfather observed while I was supping my porridge last night, that 'she was really a douce peaceable body that *Pen*.' So you perceive, my good Sir, the fault will be wholly your own, if we do not get on most harmoniously together ... But I must stop. And this is my last Letter. What a thought! How terrible and yet full of bliss. You will love me for ever, will you not, my own Husband? and I will always be your true and affectionate

    Jane Welsh

To Thomas Carlyle
Sent from Liverpool, 2 July 1844

Indeed, dear, you look to be almost unhappy enough already! I do not want you to suffer physically, only morally, you understand, and to hear of your having to take coffee at night and all that gives me *no wicked satisfaction*, but makes me quite unhappy. It is curious how much more uncomfortable I feel without you, when it is I who am going away from you, and not, as it used to be, you gone away from me. I am always wondering since I came here how I can, even in my angriest mood, talk about leaving you for good and all; for to be sure, if I were to leave you today *on that principle*, I should need absolutely to go back tomorrow *to see how you were taking it.*

George Sand
1804–76

George Sand, the pseudonym of Amandine Aurore Lucile Dupin, was born to a well-to-do French family with a country estate in Nohant near the Indre Valley. She was married at nineteen to the Baron Casimir Dudevant, but the marriage was not a happy one, and at twenty-seven she left the baron and their two children and headed for Paris, where she fell in with a group of writers including the famous critic Saint-Beuve. She published her first novel, *Indiana*, in 1832, under the pen name of George Sand (an adaptation of the name of a lover and early collaborator named Jules Sandeau). The book was an outspoken critique of the inequities of the French marriage laws at the time, and a plea for women's education and equality.

People were scandalized by George Sand's cross-dressing, her smoking (it really didn't take much) and her many love affairs. She was an astonishingly prolific writer of novels, plays and essays, and while she attracted all kinds of opprobrium for her lifestyle, her appearance and her feminist and democratic beliefs, she was obviously a deeply attractive person.

One of her most celebrated love affairs was with the

poet Alfred de Musset, who was seven years her junior. He pursued her, declaring his love for her in a famous letter of 1833, when he was twenty-two and she was twenty-nine. George allowed herself to be persuaded, and they embarked on a trip to Italy; it is not entirely clear what transpired, but the enterprise was a disaster, and their relationship ended, messily, soon afterwards. What is known is that both George and de Musset were taken ill (there is speculation that de Musset's illness was a result of his predilection for the sometimes-lethal absinthe), and George, in a fit of romantic impetuosity, fell in love with their Venetian physician, Pietro Pagello. This relationship lasted no time at all; the letter to him below might explain why, particularly George's exhortation, 'Do not learn my language, and I shall not look for, in yours, words to express my doubts and my fears. I want to be ignorant of what you do with your life and what part you play among your fellow men. I do not even want to know your name.'

After many adventures, George Sand withdrew to her family's estate in Nohant, where she lived a more tranquil life, frequently visited by her many friends from her eventful past. She died there at the age of seventy-nine.

I was in a state of shocking anxiety, my dear angel, I did not receive any letter from Antonio. I had been at Vicenza, on purpose to learn how you had passed this first night. I only heard that you had passed through the town in the morning. Thus the sole news I had about you were the two lines you wrote to me from Padua, and I did not know what to think. Pagello told me that certainly, if you were ill, Antonio would have written us; but I know that letters get lost or remain six weeks on the way in this country. I was in despair. At last I got your letter from Geneva. Oh, how I thank you for it, my child! How kind it is and how it cheered me up! Is it really true that you are not ill, that you are strong, that you do not suffer? I fear all the time that out of affection you are exaggerating your good health. Oh, may God give it you and preserve you, my *cher petit*. That is as necessary for my life henceforth as your friendship. Without the one or the other, I cannot hope for a single good day for me.

Do not believe, do not believe, Alfred, that I could be happy with the thought of having lost your heart. That I have been your mistress or your mother, what does it matter? That I have inspired you with love or with friendship – that I have been happy or unhappy with you, all that changes nothing in the state of my mind, at present. I know that I love you and that is all. [three lines erased] To watch over you, to preserve you from all ill, from all contrariety, to surround you with distractions and pleasures, that is the need and the regret which

I feel since I have lost you. Why has so sweet a task and one which I should have performed with such joy become, little by little, so bitter, and then, all at once, impossible? What fatality has changed to poison the remedies that I proffered? How is it that I, who would have offered up all my blood to give you a night's rest and peace, have become for you a torment, a scourge, a spectre? When these atrocious memories besiege me (and at what hour do they leave me in peace?), I almost go mad. I moisten my pillow with tears. I hear your voice calling to me in the silence of the night. Who will call me now? Who will have need of my watching? How shall I use up my strength that I had accumulated for you, and that now turns against me? Oh, my child, my child? How much do I not need your tenderness and your pardon! Never ask me for mine, never say that you have done me wrong. How I do know? I don't remember anything, except that we have been very unhappy and that we have parted. But I know, I feel that we shall love each other all our lives from our heart, from our intelligence, that we shall endeavour, by a sacred affection [word erased] to cure ourselves mutually from the ills we have suffered for each other.

Alas, no! it was not our fault. We obeyed our destiny, for our characters, more impulsive than others', prevented us from acquiescing in the life of ordinary lovers. But we were born to know and to love each other, be sure of that. Had it not been for thy youth and the weakness which thy tears caused me, one morning, we should have remained brother and sister . . .

Thou art right, our embraces were an incest, but we did not know it. We threw ourselves innocently and sincerely into each other's arms. Well, then, have we had a single souvenir of these embraces which was not chaste and holy? Thou hast reproached me, on a day of fever and delirium, that I never made you feel the pleasures of love. I shed tears at that, and now I am well content that there has been something true in that speech. I am well content that these pleasures have been more austere, more veiled than those you will find elsewhere. At least you will not be reminded of me in the arms of other women. But when you are alone, when you feel the need to pray and to shed tears, you will think of your George, of your true comrade, of your sick-nurse, of your friend, of something better than that. For the sentiment which unites us is combined of so many things, that it can compare to none other. The world will never understand it at all. So much the better. We love each other, and we can snap our fingers at it . . .

Adieu, adieu, my dear little child. Write me very often, I beg of you. Oh that I knew you arrived in Paris safe and sound!

Remember that you have promised me to take care of yourself. Adieu, my Alfred, love your George.

Send me, I beg of you, twelve pairs of glacé gloves, six yellow and six of colour. Send me, above all, the verses you have made. All, I have not a single one!

Born under different skies we have neither the same thoughts nor the same language – have we, perhaps, hearts that resemble one another?

The mild and cloudy climate from which I come has left me with gentle and melancholy impressions; what passions has the generous sun that has bronzed your brow given you? I know how to love and how to suffer, and you, what do you know of love?

The ardour of your glances, the violent clasp of your arms, the fervour of your desire, tempt me and frighten me. I do not know whether to combat your passion or to share it. One does not love like this in my country; beside you I am no more than a pale statue that regards you with desire, with trouble, with astonishment. I do not know if you truly love me, I shall never know it. You can scarcely speak a few words of my language and I do not know enough of yours to enter into these subtle questions. Perhaps, even if I knew perfectly the language that you speak, I should not be able to make myself understood. The place where we have lived, the people that have taught us, are, doubtless, the reason that we have ideas, sentiments and needs, inexplicable one to the other. My feeble nature and your fiery temperament must produce very different thoughts. You must be ignorant of, or despise, the thousand trivial sufferings that so disturb me; you must laugh at what makes me weep. Perhaps you even do not know what tears are. Would you be for me a support or a master? Would you console me for the evils that I have endured before meeting you? Do you understand why I am sad? Do you understand compassion, patience, friendship? Perhaps you have been brought up in the idea that women have no souls. Do you think that they have? You are neither a Christian nor a Mussulman, neither civilised nor a barbarian – are you a man? What is there in that masculine bosom, behind that superb brow, those leonine eyes? Do you ever have a nobler, finer thought, a fraternal pious sentiment? When you sleep, do you dream that you are flying towards Heaven? When men wrong you do you still trust in God? Shall I be your companion or your slave? Do you desire me or love me? When your passion is satisfied will you thank me? When I have made you happy, will you know how to tell me so? Do you know what I am and does it trouble you not to know it? Am I for you an unknown being who must be sought for and dreamt of, or am I in your eyes a woman like those that fatten in harems? In your eyes, in which I think to see a divine spark, is there nothing but a lust such as these women inspire? Do you know that desire of the soul that time does not quench, that no excess deadens or wearies? When your mistress sleeps in your arms, do you stay awake to watch over her, to pray to God and to weep? Do the pleasures of love leave you breathless and brutalised or do they throw you into a divine ecstasy? Does your soul overcome your body when you leave the bosom of her whom you love? Ah, when I shall observe you withdrawn quiet, shall I know if you are thoughtful or at rest? When your glance is languishing will it be tenderness or lassitude? Perhaps you realise that I do not know you and that you do not know me. I know neither your past life, nor your character, nor what the men that know you think of you. Perhaps you are the first, perhaps the last among them. I love you without knowing if I can esteem you, I love you because you please me, and perhaps some day I shall be forced to hate you. If you were a man of my country, I should question you and you would understand me. But perhaps I should be still more unhappy, for you would mislead me. As it is, at least you will not deceive me, you will make no vain promises and false vows. You will love me as you understand love, as you can love. What I have sought for in vain in others, I shall not, perhaps, find in you, but I can always believe that you possess it. Those looks, those caresses of love that have always lied to me in others, you will allow me to interpret as I wish, without adding deceitful words to them. I shall be able to interpret your reveries and fill your silences with eloquence. I shall give to your actions the intentions that I wish them to have. When you look at me tenderly, I shall believe that your soul is gazing at mine; when you glance at heaven, I shall believe that your mind turns towards the eternity from which it sprang. Let us remain thus, do not learn my language, and I shall not look for, in yours, words to express my doubts and my fears. I want to be ignorant of what you do with your life and what part you play among your fellow men. I do not even want to know your name. Hide your soul from me that I may always believe it to be beautiful.

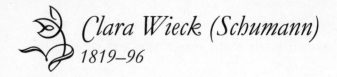

Clara Wieck (Schumann)
1819–96

Clara Wieck was born in Leipzig, daughter of the renowned piano teacher Friedrich Wieck and Marianne Tromlitz, a soprano and former pupil of Wieck's. Clara was a child prodigy, and her ambitious father devised a special programme for her, with daily lessons in piano, violin, singing, harmony, composition and counterpoint; she gave her first public recital in Leipzig at the age of nine. She first met her future husband, Robert Schumann, when he came to study with her father in 1830. Robert was a gifted pianist, but an injury to his hand meant that he could never fulfil his promise; instead, he became a composer and influential critic.

Clara toured Europe with her father between 1831 and 1835 and was also working on her own compositions. She was recognized as a virtuoso throughout France and Germany when Schumann began his courtship of her in the mid 1830s, and in 1837 he proposed marriage – below is her response. But Friedrich withheld his consent, and three years of bitter dispute followed. Eventually, the couple obtained permission from the Court of Appeals in Leipzig to marry, and their wedding took place in 1840, the day before Clara was twenty-one. In the light of later events, one must wonder whether Friedrich saw in the intense young man signs of the mental instability which would blight his later life. This was also the year that Robert composed more than a hundred of his famous *Lieder*.

Between 1841 and 1854, Clara Schumann gave birth to eight children, one of whom died in infancy. The family travelled all over Europe, with Clara showcasing Robert's compositions, and in 1850 they settled in Düsseldorf, where he became director of the city's orchestra.

Robert first suffered from depression and delusions in 1844; he recovered, but relapsed in 1854 and tried to drown himself in the Rhine while Clara was pregnant with their eighth child. He was rescued, but committed to an asylum, where he died two years later.

Clara survived her husband by forty years, bringing up her children alone, four of whom she also outlived. For the rest of her life she taught, gave recitals all over Europe and devoted herself to burnishing her late husband's reputation as a composer. She gave her last public concert in 1891 at the age of seventy-two, and died after suffering a stroke in 1896.

It is only relatively recently that Clara Schumann's

own reputation as a composer has been re-evaluated; although she was writing music from an early age, she seemed to lose her confidence as she grew older, saying, 'I once believed that I possessed creative talent, but I have given up this idea; a woman must not desire to compose – there has never yet been one able to do it. Should I expect to be the one?'

To Robert Schumann
Sent from Leipzig, 15 August 1837

You require but a simple 'Yes'? Such a small word – but such an important one. But should not a heart so full of unutterable love as mine utter this little word with all its might? I do so and my innermost soul whispers always to you.

The sorrows of my heart, the many tears, could I depict them to you – oh no! Perhaps fate will ordain that we see each other soon and then – your intention seems risky to me and yet a loving heart does not take much count of dangers. But once again I say to you 'Yes'. Would God make my eighteenth birthday a day of woe? Oh no! that would be too horrible. Besides I have long felt 'it must be', nothing in the world shall persuade me to stray from what I think right and I will show my father that the youngest of hearts can also be steadfast in purpose.

Your Clara

Queen Victoria
1819–1901

Victoria was the only child of Edward, Duke of Kent, the fourth son of George III, and Princess Victoire of Saxe-Coburg-Saalfeld; her father died in 1820, and she was brought up in near isolation at Kensington Palace. She was permitted to know of her probable destiny at the age of ten – the occasion on which, according to legend, she exclaimed, 'I will be good!' She succeeded to the throne in 1837, when she was eighteen.

That same year Victoria was introduced to her cousin Prince Albert of Saxe-Coburg and Gotha, a match much wished for by her mother, but the new young queen was enjoying her first taste of independence, and in no hurry to change her circumstances. It wasn't until Albert presented himself again in 1839 that she fell in love with him. Victoria, as queen, had to propose to Albert, which must have been the occasion for some awkwardness, but he accepted and they were married on 10 February 1840.

Victoria's character – headstrong, stubborn, sociable – was transformed by marriage. Albert compensated for his wife's superior status with an absolute rule in the domestic sphere, and his punishment for wifely transgressions was a withdrawal of affection. Victoria, terrified of losing the husband upon whom she was increasingly reliant, would submit, and harmony would be restored. His letters, formerly addressed to 'Beloved Victoria', now began, 'Dear Child'. And of course the balance of power shifted as the couple began to reproduce; between 1840 and 1857 Victoria gave birth to nine children, all of whom, unusually for the time, survived to adulthood.

By the 1840s, Albert was joint monarch in all but name – and the fact that he had no official title was a constant source of fretful regret to Victoria. She tried in 1854 and again in 1856 to have him declared prince consort by Parliament; when her second attempt failed, she conferred the title upon him herself.

Albert was consulted by his wife in all matters of state, and she followed his direction. On his own account, he oversaw the construction of new royal homes at Balmoral in Scotland and Osborne House on the Isle of Wight, and supervised the triumphant Great Exhibition at Crystal Palace in 1851. It is impossible to overstate how much Victoria depended on her husband; her children were a distant second in her affections, and she would do nothing without his express approval. When he died in 1861, probably of stomach cancer, she was utterly inconsolable, and plunged the court into a mourning so deep as to be quite spectacular even by the stringent standards of the time. She declared, '*his* wishes—*his* plans—about everything, *his* views about *every* thing are to be *my law*! And no human power will make me swerve from what he decided and wished.' She did not emerge again into the public gaze until 1872, and even then it was only at the urging of her most senior advisers, who feared that republicanism was gaining a real foothold among the populace.

Victoria is a fascinating character: wilful yet entirely submissive to her husband; politically partisan to an alarming degree, but swayed by idiosyncratic personal likes and dislikes; avowedly anti-suffrage (having no truck with the '*socalled & most erroneous* "Rights of, Woman"', as she wrote to one of her prime ministers) yet wielding more power than any other woman in the world, and relishing the title of 'Victoria *regina et imperatrix*' (Victoria, queen and empress). She died in 1901, having celebrated her diamond jubilee. The queen believed it undignified to smile in portraits and photographs (much like today's Victoria *regina et imperatrix*, Mrs Beckham), and the image of the tiny (four foot eleven), dumpy, severe-looking woman swathed in black has become iconic, but there is a photograph taken in 1898 by Charles Knight in which she is caught off guard, smiling, and her entire aspect is transformed.

The first letter below was written to Albert ten days before their wedding. It reveals Victoria in her 'before' state, when she feels quite at ease asserting her authority over her husband-to-be; he has been lobbying for a long honeymoon in the country, and Victoria reminds him in no uncertain terms that her business lies in London. This state of affairs lasted a very short time indeed. The second letter, to her uncle King Leopold, gives some indication of her devastation after his death.

To Prince Albert
Sent from Buckingham Palace, 31 January 1840

. . . You have written to me in one of your letters about our stay at Windsor, but, dear Albert, you have not at all understood the matter. *You forget, my dearest Love, that I am the Sovereign, and that business can stop and wait for nothing. Parliament is sitting, and something occurs almost every day, for which I may be required, and it is quite impossible for me to be absent from London; therefore two or three days is already a long time to be absent. I am never easy a moment, if I am not on the spot, and see and hear what is going on, and everybody, including all my Aunts (who are very knowing in all these things), says I must come out after the second day, for, as I must be surrounded by my Court, I cannot keep alone. This is also my own wish in every way.*

Now as to the Arms: *as an English Prince you have no right, and Uncle Leopold had no right to quarter the English Arms, but the Sovereign has the power to allow it by Royal Command: this was done for Uncle Leopold by the Prince Regent, and I will do it again for you. But it can only be done by Royal Command.*

I will, therefore, without delay, have a seal engraved for you . . . I read in the newspaper that you, dear Albert, have received many Orders; also that the Queen of Spain will send you the Golden Fleece . . .

Farewell, dearest Albert, and think often of thy faithful Victoria R.

*To the King of the Belgians
Sent from Osborne, 20 December 1861*

MY *own* DEAREST, KINDEST *FATHER*, – For as such have I *ever* loved you! The poor fatherless baby of eight months is now the utterly broken-hearted and crushed widow of forty-two! My *life* as a *happy* one is *ended!* the world is gone for *me!* If I *must live* on (and I will do nothing to make me worse than I am), it is henceforth for our poor fatherless children – for my unhappy country, which has lost *all* in losing him – and in *only* doing what I know and *feel* he would wish, for he *is* near me – his spirit will guide and inspire me!

But oh! to be cut off in the prime of life – to see our pure, happy, quiet, domestic life, which *alone* enabled me to bear my *much* disliked position, CUT OFF at forty-two – when I *had* hoped with such instinctive certainty that God never *would* part us, and would let us grow old together (though *he* always talked of the shortness of life) – is *too awful*, too cruel! And yet it *must* be for *his* good, his happiness! His purity was too great, his aspiration *too high* for this poor, *miserable* world! His great soul is *now only* enjoying *that* for which it *was* worthy! And I will *not* envy him – only pray that *mine* may be perfected by it and fit to be with him eternally, for which blessed moment I earnestly long. Dearest, dearest Uncle, *how* kind of you to come! It will be an unspeakable *comfort*, and you *can do* much to tell people to do what they ought to do. As for my *own good, personal* servants – poor Phipps in particular – nothing can be more devoted, heart-broken as they are, and anxious only to live as *he* wished!

Good Alice has been and is wonderful.

The 26th will suit me perfectly. Ever your devoted, wretched Child,

Victoria R.

Emily Dickinson
1830–86

Emily Dickinson, one of the greatest poets of the nineteenth century, was born into a prominent Massachusetts family; her grandfather was a founder of Amherst College; her father was its treasurer and served in the General Court of Massachusetts, the State Senate and the House of Representatives. She had an elder brother, Austin, and a younger sister, Lavinia.

Emily was educated at Amherst Academy and then spent a year at the South Hadley Female Seminary, now Mount Holyoke College. In 1848 having spent just a year at the seminary, she returned to her family's house, known locally as the Homestead, where she lived for the rest of her life. Her only forays beyond Amherst were a trip to Washington, DC, to Philadelphia, and a few trips to Boston. She started writing poems in her early twenties, fitting her work around her domestic duties at the Homestead.

Emily Dickinson's withdrawal from all but her family's society seems to have been a gradual process, but it coincided with her most productive period as a poet in the early 1860s. Her most important literary mentor was Thomas Wentworth Higginson, a writer and radical. After he published an article giving advice to young writers in the *Atlantic* in 1862, Emily wrote to him enclosing some of her work. He was encouraging (if a little taken aback by what seemed to him the idiosyncratic style of the poems), and their correspondence lasted for the rest of her life (they met once, in Amherst, in 1870).

One of Emily Dickinson's closest relationships was with Susan Gilbert, whom she met as a girl at the Amherst Academy, and to whom she wrote more than three hundred letters. In 1856, after a four-year courtship, Susan married Emily's brother Austin, and the couple built a house next to the Homestead which they called the Evergreens. Their marriage was unhappy, but they lived there, together, for the rest of Emily's life.

Emily Dickinson's circumscribed existence in Amherst has left a sketchy biography – fertile ground for impertinent speculation and half-baked psycho-analysis. What is beyond dispute is that her reclusive life left her free to write almost 1,800 poems, only a handful of which were published before she died in 1886, but which eventually changed for ever the way people think about poetry.

After her death, more than forty 'fascicles' were

discovered in her room – manuscript books of poems that Emily had assembled and sewn herself. Various selections were published (some edited by Thomas Wentworth Higginson) between 1890 and 1935, but these versions were heavily reworked to conform with contemporary ideas about how poetry should look. It wasn't until 1955 that *The Poems of Emily Dickinson* appeared; edited by Thomas H. Johnson, it restored Emily Dickinson's revolutionary syntax, capitalization and punctuation, and finally revealed her true genius.

To Susan Gilbert (Dickinson), 6 February 1852

Will you let me come dear Susie – looking just as I do, my dress soiled and worn, my grand old apron, and my hair – Oh Susie, time would fail me to enumerate my appearance, yet I love you just as dearly as if I was e'er so fine, so you wont care, will you? I am so glad dear Susie – that our hearts are always clean, and always neat and lovely, so not to be ashamed. I have been hard at work this morning, and I ought to be working now – but I cannot deny myself the luxury of a minute or two with you.

The dishes may wait dear Susie – and the uncleared table stand, *them* I have always with me, but you, I have 'not always' – *why* Susie, Christ hath saints *manie* – and I have *few*, but thee – the angels shant have Susie – no – no no!

Vinnie is sewing away like a *fictitious* seamstress, and I half expect some knight will arrive at the door, confess himself a *nothing* in presence of her loveliness, and present his heart and hand as the only vestige of him worthy to be refused.

Vinnie and I have been talking about growing old, today. Vinnie thinks *twenty* must be a fearful position for one to occupy – I tell her I don't care if I am young or not, had as lief be thirty, and you, as most anything else. Vinnie expresses her sympathy at my 'sere and yellow leaf' and resumes her work, dear Susie, tell me how *you* feel – ar'nt there days in one's life when to be old dont seem a thing so sad –

I do feel gray and grim, this morning, and I feel it would be a comfort to have a piping voice, and broken back, and scare little children. Dont *you* run, Susie dear, for I wont do any harm, and I do love you dearly tho' I do feel so frightful.

Oh my darling one, how long you wander from me, how weary I grow of waiting and looking, and calling for you; sometimes I shut my eyes, and shut my heart towards you, and try hard to forget you because you grieve me so, but you'll never go away, Oh you never will – say, Susie, promise me again, and I will smile faintly – and take up my little cross again of sad – *sad* separation. How vain it seems to *write*, when one knows how to feel – how much more near and dear to sit beside you, talk with you, hear the tones of your voice; so hard to 'deny thyself, and take up thy cross, and follow me' – give me strength, Susie, write me of hope and love, and of hearts that *endured*, and great was their reward of 'Our Father who art in Heaven'. I don't know how I shall bear it, when the gentle spring comes; if she should come and see me and talk to me of you, Oh it would surely kill me! While the frost clings to the windows, and the World is stern and drear; this absence is easier; the *Earth* mourns too, for all her little birds; but when they all come back again, and she sings and is so merry – pray what will become of me? Susie, forgive me, forget all what I say, get some sweet little scholar to read a gentle hymn, about Bethleem and Mary, and you will sleep on sweetly and have as peaceful dreams, as if I had never written you all these ugly things. Never mind the letter Susie, I wont be angry with you if you don't give me any at all – for I know how busy you are, and how little of that dear strength remains when it is evening, with which to think and write. Only *want* to write me, only sometimes sigh that you are far from me, and that will do, Susie! Dont you think we are good and patient, to let you go so long; and don't we think you're a darling, a real beautiful hero, to toil for people, and teach them, and leave your own dear home? Because we pine and repine, dont think we forget the precious patriot at war in other lands! Never be mournful Susie – be happy and have cheer, for how many of the long days have gone away since I wrote you – and it is almost noon, and soon the night will come, and then there is one less day of the long pilgrimage. Mattie is very smart, talks of you *much*, my darling; I must leave you now – 'one little hour of Heaven,' thank who did give it me, and will he also grant me one longer and *more* when it shall please his love – bring Susie home, ie! Love always, and ever, and true!

    Emily

Isabella Mayson (Mrs Beeton)
1836–65

Isabella Mayson was born off Cheapside in the City of London, the eldest of four children. Her father, Benjamin Mayson, a linen merchant, died when she was four, and in 1843 her mother, Elizabeth, married Henry Dorling, who was the Clerk of the Course at Epsom. Henry was a widower with four children, so the couple began married life with a brood of eight; to this were added a further, scarcely credible, thirteen children over the next twenty years, making Isabella the eldest of twenty-one siblings, half-siblings and step-siblings. It is hardly surprising that she became a dab hand at household management.

Isabella was educated in Heidelberg, where her studies focused on music and languages, and where she also discovered her skill as a pastry chef, which she continued to practise for an Epsom confectioner when she returned there in 1854.

In 1856, Isabella married Samuel Orchart Beeton, a book and magazine publisher who had had an early success with the publication of *Uncle Tom's Cabin* by the abolitionist Harriet Beecher Stowe. Among Samuel's stable of periodicals was the *English Woman's*

Domestic Magazine, a twopenny monthly. Mrs Beeton became active in her husband's business almost straight away, and by 1859 was 'editress' of the *Domestic Magazine*. She was a great innovator – she returned from a visit to Paris with the idea of including a fashion plate in each issue, and a pattern service for readers; these features became staples of women's magazines for the next century.

The achievement for which Mrs Beeton's name is renowned was of course *Mrs Beeton's Book of Household Management*, which was published as a part-work between 1859 and 1861, then as an illustrated volume, followed by numerous mass-market editions. Mrs Beeton set out her stall in her introduction: 'I have always thought that there is no more fruitful source of family discontent than a housewife's badly-cooked dinners and untidy ways.' Aimed at the emerging Victorian middle class, *Household Management* was much, much more than a collection of recipes; it covered every aspect of the domestic sphere, including budgeting, the management of servants, etiquette (on finger bowls: 'The French and other continentals have a habit of gargling the mouth; but it is a custom which no English gentlewoman should, in the slightest degree, imitate'), hygiene, dress, first aid, childcare and even legal matters pertaining to buying a house, taking a tenancy, letting and insuring property and the drawing up of a will. *Household Management* is a monumental work, which now provides a riveting picture of middle-class Victorian women's lives; for its original readers though, especially newly married women, it must have been an absolutely indispensable guide to navigating all aspects of everyday life.

During the time that Isabella was compiling *Household Management*, she gave birth to four sons, two of whom died: one in his first year, the other at the age of three. Isabella died of peritonitis and puerperal fever eight days after giving birth to her fourth son, Mayson, in February 1865 at the terribly young age of twenty-eight. Samuel outlived her by only twelve years, succumbing to tuberculosis at the age of forty-seven. That his happy and immensely productive partnership with his wife lasted only eight and a half years, coupled with the death of their first two children, must have been a source of immense sadness to him.

To Sam Beeton
Sent from Epsom, 26 May 1856

My own darling Sam,

As I have two or three little matters in your note of yesterday that rather puzzled me, I thought I must write and ask
an explanation; very stupid of me you will say, as I am going
to see you on Wednesday morning. No doubt you will think
that I could just as well have [asked you] myself then, as
trouble you with one of my unintelligible epistles . . .

Secondly, what right has he to conjure up in his fertile
brain such nasty things as rough corners to smooth down
when there is one who loves him better and more fondly
than ever one being did another, on this earth at least.

Oh Sam, I think it is so wrong of you to fancy such
dreadful things. You say also you don't think I shall be able
to guide myself when I am left to my own exertions. I must
say, I have always looked up to, and respected, both parents
and perhaps been mindful of what they say (I mean respect-
ing certain matters) but in a very short time you will have the
entire management of me and I can assure you that you will
find in me a most docile and yielding pupil.

Pray don't imagine when I am yours – that things will
continue as they are now. God forbid. Better would it be to
put an end to this matter altogether if we thought there was
the slightest possibility of *that*. So pray don't tremble for our
future happiness.

Look at things in a more rosy point of view and I have

no doubt with the love *I am sure* there is existing between us, we shall get on as merrily as crickets with only an occasionally sharp point to soften down and not as many as you fancy . . .

I could not sleep without writing to you, so you must excuse this nonsense. Good-night my precious pet, may angels guide and watch over you and give you pleasant dreams, not drab colours, and accept the fondest and most sincere love of your

Bella

Burn this as soon as read.

Mary Wyndham (Lady Elcho)
1862–1937

Mary Wyndham was born in Belgravia into a family both aristocratic and artistic; her father was a patron of the pre-Raphaelites, and the family home was filled with painters, poets and writers. She was educated at home by a governess, and in 1883 the stunningly beautiful young woman (she was painted by both Edward Poynder and Sargent) was persuaded by her family to marry Hugo Richard Charteris, Lord Elcho. Charteris was a charmer, but a wastrel; the marriage was not happy, and Mary was often left alone with the children (seven were born between 1884 and 1902). But while she had failed to fall in love with Hugo, she had fallen in love with the house her father-in-law gave them as a wedding present: Stanway, in Gloucestershire, a fine Jacobean manor built of honey-coloured Cotswold stone, surrounded by beautiful grounds containing a spectacular eighteenth-century water garden and a fourteenth-century tithe barn. The house became a focal point for all sorts of gatherings – Mary was one of the legendary hostesses of the age – but most particularly the unofficial headquarters of a group that became known as 'the Souls'. In some ways a precursor to the Bloomsbury set, the Souls eschewed the usual aristocratic pastimes – tramping about shooting things and a fanatical interest in horse racing – in favour of conversation, music and word games. One of its leading lights was Arthur Balfour, then a backbench Unionist MP, who later became prime minister.

Balfour never married, and doesn't appear to have been particularly interested in sex. But the languid, intellectual and usually uncommunicative philosopher-politician found in Mary someone in whom he could confide; she in turn found the kindred spirit her husband clearly was not. Margot Asquith, a fellow Soul, claimed that Balfour was never in love, citing as evidence his response when she asked him if he would mind if she, Mary and another of their friends were all to die: 'I would mind if you all died on the same *day*.'

The friendship and correspondence between Mary and Balfour lasted for forty years until his death in 1930. She was evidently a woman of energy and wit, who for most of her life was locked in a loveless marriage, although in 1895 she embarked on an adventure to Egypt where she had an affair with the explorer Wilfrid Scawen Blunt and returned pregnant – her husband accepted the child as his own in keeping with the aristocratic custom of the time. In 1914 Hugo inherited his father's title and grand estate in East Lothian, where he decamped to live in splendour with his mistress. Mary managed to stay on at Stanway only through the charity of the playwright James Barrie. She lost two sons in the First World War, and as a memorial she wrote the story of their lives, *A Family Record*, which was published in 1932. Mary Charteris lived out her days at Stanway, and died in a nearby nursing home in 1937.

To Arthur Balfour
Written on a train between Oxford and Warwick,
19 January 1904

I was overwhelmed with depression at leaving you Sunday night, and I think you looked rather sad too which – this sounds unkind – was rather a consolation. It was horrid leaving at that hour but practically it was unavoidable so 'there's nothing to regret' in *that* sense (this is a Whitt phrase) except that it had to be done and I think it was quite clever of me to fit in everything so well and manage to get to you – you see, I felt it my duty to put you in *yr place* (on yr knees at my feet) and *that* I flatter myself I have thoroughly done. Sunday was a little disappointing, because altho' my conscience wanted you to go to church I *should* have liked to have had some fun with you in the morning. I was in great spirits and full of mischief when you rushed in. (by the way, how *awful* of you to leave my letter in yr room) then came the long walk and one hour in yr room seemed very little in all the day and it was wasted in talking business. 2 hrs is what I like: one for boring things and one for putting you in yr place: I know I dwell too much on each thing and the more I fancy you're bored the more gingerly I go, which is quite wrong. I hate rushing but it ought to be done as time is short. Then the interval between tea and dinner and departure was a great strain because I felt I wanted so to see you alone and kept *wondering* if it could be managed, certainly not unless I had arranged it beforehand – impossible to get yr attention, I thought of yr showing me something or fetching something in yr room. Eventually I gave it up and mental and physical spirits went down like a pricked balloon. I had some of my pain in my side. The motor drive was very nice but not so much fun *going away* in it. I tipped Mills . . .

I wish I had a motor. I forgot to tell you that Tuesday 6th would suit me best: I should like a clear week at Stanway but you must settle what pleases you.

Goodbye. Bless you.

ME

I hope you are all right? Destroy.

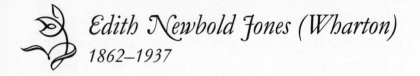

Edith Newbold Jones (Wharton)
1862–1937

Edith Wharton was born Edith Newbold Jones to a prominent New York society family who had made their fortune in shipping, banking and real estate. She was brought up in a brownstone on 23rd Street, just off Park Avenue, and was educated by governesses and by reading in her father's library. Edith seems to have been a born storyteller, and had completed her first (never published) novel by the age of fifteen.

Her mother, Lucretia, a doyenne of grand New York society, was anxious that this clever, bookish daughter find a husband; in 1885, she married Edward 'Teddy' Robbins Wharton, a friend of her brother's. A Bostonian, Teddy shared the moneyed, leisured lifestyle of his new wife's family, but sadly he had nothing at all in common with his wife in terms of temperament or interests.

Edith Wharton's struggle to reconcile her position as a society matron with her creative impulse meant that after her youthful flurry of productivity, she produced no further fiction until she was thirty-eight. In the meantime, her annual trips to Europe inspired her to write about art, architecture, gardens and interior design. Her first published book was *The Decoration of Houses*, co-written with the designer Ogden Codman, an argument in favour of a more classically elegant, restrained and simple style than the prevailing fashion for mammoth furnishings, dark colour schemes and clutter.

Her first bestselling novel, *The House of Mirth*, about the old New York society in which she had grown up, was published in 1905. Edith was by then living for most of the year in western Massachusetts in a classical villa of her own design called the Mount, while Teddy Wharton appeared to be increasingly in the grip of mental illness. A friend of Edith's wrote, 'Mr Wharton's mania leads him to buy houses and motors for music-hall actresses, to engage huge suites in hotels and get drunk and break all the furniture and to circulate horrible tales about his wife.'

In 1907, Henry James, who had become Edith's close friend, introduced her to Morton Fullerton, a Bostonian who had become Paris correspondent for the London *Times*. She fell in love with him and moved to Paris full time. Again she had chosen badly; Fullerton was a bisexual divorcé who was being blackmailed by a former mistress over his homosexual past and was involved in a quasi-incestuous affair with his cousin, who had grown up in his parents' household.

Teddy at least had the excuse of mental disorder for his appalling behaviour; Fullerton appears to have been an out-and-out opportunist, more or less a living definition of the word 'cad'. The affair between Edith and Fullerton lasted on and off until 1911. It is possible that when Fullerton realized Edith was moving towards divorcing the increasingly erratic Teddy, he thought it expedient to back off.

For the rest of her life Edith lived in France. She received the Legion of Honour for her war work, raising funds and establishing hostels for French and Belgian refugees, and also became a war correspondent, reporting from the front line back to the United States. In 1921, she received a Pulitzer Prize for *The Age of Innocence*, and in 1923 took an honorary doctorate in letters from Yale University. In 1930 she was elected to the American Academy of Arts and Letters. She died in 1937 at her house in Pavillon Colombe, just north of Paris. She is often described as a 'society novelist' or 'a novelist of manners' – both phrases carry with them a hint of the pejorative. She was an astonishingly astute and open-minded writer with a forensic eye for human fallibility, whose themes and interests ranged far beyond the drawing rooms of Old New York.

To W. Morton Fullerton
Sent from 58 rue de Varenne, March 1908

Dear, Remember, please, how impatient & anxious I shall
be to know the sequel of the Bell letter . . .

—Do you know what I was thinking last night, when you
asked me, & I couldn't tell you? —Only that the way you've
spent your emotional life, while I've — bien malgré moi —
hoarded mine, is what puts the great gulf between us, &
sets us not only on opposite shores, but at hopelessly distant points of our respective shores . . . Do you see what I
mean?

And I'm so afraid that the treasures I long to unpack for
you, that have come to me in magic ships from enchanted
islands, are only, to you, the old familiar red calico & beads
of the clever trader who has had dealings in every latitude,
& knows just what to carry in the hold to please the simple
native — I'm so afraid of this, that often & often I stuff my
shining treasures back into their box, lest I should see you
smiling at them!

Well! And if you do? It's *your* loss, after all! And if you
can't come into the room without my feeling all over me a
ripple of flame, & if, wherever you touch me, a heart beats
under your touch, & if, when you hold me, & I don't speak,
it's because all the words in me seem to have become throb-
bing pulses, & all my thoughts are a great golden blur — why
should I be afraid of your smiling at me, when I can turn
the beads & calico back into such beauty— ?

Rosa Luxemburg
1871–1919

Rosa Luxemburg was born in Zamość, near Lublin, in Russian-controlled Poland, the fifth child of a timber merchant. She was educated in Poland and in 1886 joined the Polish Proletariat Party. By 1889, she was so notorious as a political agitator that she had to flee from Poland to Zürich, Switzerland, to escape imprisonment. She continued her studies at the University of Zürich, taking her doctorate in 1898. It was there that she met Leo Jogiches, with whom she founded the Social Democratic Party of the Kingdom of Poland. Rosa and Leo had a long love affair but never really lived together; their politics were, ultimately, more important to both of them than domestic happiness.

In 1898 Rosa married Karl Lübeck, the son of a friend, in order to move to Berlin. The two main strands of her political thought can be identified as a scepticism about nationalism – her cause was socialist revolution across Europe, rather than individual nations acting alone – and a conviction that revolution, not reform, was the only way of bringing freedom to the masses.

Once in Germany, Rosa began agitating against

German militarism and imperialism and constantly found herself in trouble with the authorities, often for inciting mass strike action. In June 1916, as she tried to lead an anti-war strike, she was arrested and imprisoned for two and a half years. When the authorities reluctantly released her in 1918, she and her comrades immediately founded the German Communist Party and a newspaper called the *Red Flag*. In January 1919, amid scenes of revolutionary chaos in Berlin, Rosa was arrested by the so-called *Freikorps*, bands of paramilitaries associated with the right-wing movements which were beginning to gather momentum. She was taken to a hotel and beaten until she was unconscious; her body was then dumped in the Landwehr Canal. Her murder has been described as the first triumph of Nazi Germany.

The letter below to Leo Jogiches contains arguably one of the most poignant (and, it must be said, amusing) effusions in this collection: thanking him for the gift of a book, Rosa writes, 'You simply cannot imagine how pleased I am with your choice. Why, Rodbertus is simply my favourite economist.' (Rodbertus worked primarily on the labour theory of value.) This might go some way towards illustrating how the relationship between Luxemburg and Jogiches never became the first priority for either of them, despite the love they may have felt for each other.

To Leo Jogiches, 6 March 1899

I kiss you a thousand times for your dearest letter and present, though I have not yet received it . . . You simply cannot imagine how pleased I am with your choice. Why, Rodbertus is simply my favourite economist and I can read him a hundred times for sheer intellectual pleasure . . . My dear, how you delighted me with your letter. I have read it six times from beginning to end. So, you are really pleased with me. You write that perhaps I only know inside me that somewhere there is a man who belongs to me! Don't you know that everything I do is always done with you in mind: when I write an article my first thought is – will this cause you pleasure – and when I have days when I doubt my own strength and cannot work, my only fear is what effect this will have on you, that it might disappoint you. When I have proof of success, like a letter from Kautsky, this is simply my homage to you. I give you my word, as I loved my mother, that I am personally quite indifferent to what Kautsky writes. I was only pleased with it because I wrote it with your eyes and felt how much pleasure it would give you.

. . . Only one thing nags at my contentment: the outward arrangements of your life and of our relationship. I feel that

I will soon have such an established position (morally) that we will be able to live together quite calmly, openly, as husband and wife. I am sure you understand this yourself. I am happy that the problem of your citizenship is at last coming to an end and that you are working energetically at your doctorate. I can feel from your recent letters that you are in a very good mood to work . . .

Do you think that I do not feel your value, that whenever the call to arms is sounded you always stand by me with help and encourage me to work – forgetting all the rows and all my neglect!

. . . You have no idea with what joy and desire I wait for every letter from you because each one brings me so much strength and happiness and encourages me to live.

I was happiest of all with that part of your letter where you write that we are both young and can still arrange our personal life. Oh darling, how I long that you may fulfil your promise . . . Our own little room, our furniture, a library of our own, quiet and regular work, walks together, an opera from time to time, a small – very small – circle of intimate friends who can sometimes be asked to dinner, every year a summer departure to the country for a month but definitely free from work! . . . And perhaps even a little, a very little, baby? Will this never be permitted? Never? Darling, do you know what accosted me yesterday during a walk in the park – and without any exaggeration? A little child, three or four years old, in a beautiful dress with blond hair; it stared at me and suddenly I felt an overpowering urge to kidnap the child and dash off home with him. Oh darling, will I never have my own baby?

And at home we will never argue again, will we? It must be quiet and peaceful as it is with everyone else. Only you know what worries me, I feel already so old and am not in the least attractive. You will not have an attractive wife when you walk hand in hand with her through the park – we will keep well away from the Germans . . . Darling, if you will first settle the question of your citizenship, secondly your doctorate and thirdly live with me openly in our own room and work together with me, then we can want for nothing more! No couple on earth has so many facilities for happiness as you and I and if there is only some goodwill on our part we will be, must be, happy.

Empress Alexandra of Russia
1872–1918

Alexandra's mother was Princess Alice, the second daughter of Queen Victoria; her father was Prince Louis of the Grand Duchy of Hesse. Princess Alice was energetic and forward-thinking and a great philanthropist with a particular interest in the education and training of women. She died of diphtheria following a visit to a hospital when Alexandra was only six.

Alexandra and Nicholas, the Tsarevich of Russia, had fallen in love against the opposition both of Queen Victoria and of Nicholas's father, the Tsar. But with the Tsar in failing health, the objections were eventually overcome. He died on 1 November 1894; later that month, Nicholas and Alexandra were married and Alexandra became Tsarina. But life at the Russian court proved problematic. The people suspected her of being pro-German – which became an even more serious problem with the outbreak of the First World War; the nobility thought her insufficiently grand to have become empress; and her mother-in-law, the Dowager Empress, did everything she could to undermine her, including openly sneering at the fact that after ten years of marriage she had produced only daughters. Finally, in 1904, she gave birth to Alexei, the Tsarevich. Her joy and relief must have turned to anguish when she realized that he had inherited haemophilia, an often fatal condition at the time. The knowledge that it had been passed down from her side of the family – Queen Victoria was a carrier – must have made it even more difficult to bear.

In despair over the fragile health of her son, with doctors who were unable to offer any help, Alexandra turned to an array of healers, seers and mystics, the most notorious of whom was Rasputin, a kind of non-aligned monk of shady background and no credentials. Photographs show a greasy-haired, long-bearded middle-aged man striking a quasi-religious pose in the apparent belief that a mad, staring facial expression is the mark of a true mystic. Rasputin became, if possible, even more unpopular with both the people and the nobility than Alexandra herself, and was murdered by a gang of courtiers in 1916.

From some accounts of Alexandra's relationship with this charlatan, one might think she was single-handedly responsible for the Russian Revolution. But by 1917, the country was on its knees: famine was widespread, the mismanaged war dragged on, soldiers were opening fire on protestors and the Tsar – completely backed up by Alexandra, as can be seen below – refused to contemplate any kind of constitutional reform. After the February revolution Nicholas was forced to abdicate. He and his family were imprisoned by the Bolsheviks in various locations, and finally taken to a house at Ekaterinburg in the Urals. There, in the middle of the night of 16–17 July 1918, the entire family and three servants were taken by their guards from their sleeping quarters to the basement where, in a bloody chaos of bullets and bayonets, they were all killed.

To Tsar Nicholas II

Lovy dear, my telegrams can't be very warm, as they go through so many military hands – but you will read all my love and longing between the lines. Sweety, if in any way you do not feel quite the thing, you will be sure to call Feodorov, won't you – & have an eye on Fredericks.

My very most earnest prayers will follow you by day and night. I commend you into our Lord's safe keeping – may He guard, guide & lead you & bring you safe & sound back again.

I bless you & love you, as man has rarely been loved

before – & kiss every dearly beloved place & press you tenderly to my own heart.

For ever yr. Very own old
Wify

The Image will lie this night under my cushion before I give it to you with my fervent blessing.

To Tsar Nicholas II
Sent from Tsarskoje Selo, 4 December 1916

My Very Precious One,
Good-bye, sweet Lovy!

Its great pain to let you go – worse than ever after the hard times we have been living & fighting through. But God who is all love & mercy has let the things take a change for the better, – just a little more patience & deepest faith in the prayers & help of our Friend – then all will go well. I am fully convinced that great & beautiful times are coming for yr. Reign & Russia. Only keep up your spirits, let no talks or letters pull you down – let them pass by as something unclean & quickly to be forgotten.

Show to all, that you are the Master & your will shall be obeyed – the time of great indulgence & gentleness is over – now comes your reign of will & power, & they shall be made to bow down before you & listen to your orders & to work how & with whom you wish – obedience they must be taught, they do not know the meaning of that word, you have spoilt them by yr. kindness & all forgivingness.

Why do people hate me? Because they know I have a strong will & when am convinced of a thing being right (when besides blessed by *Gregory*), do not change my mind & that they can't bear. But its the bad ones.

Remember Mr Phillips words when he gave me the image with the bell. As you were so kind, trusting & gentle, I was to be yr. bell, those that came with wrong intentions wld. not be able to approach me & I wld. warn you. Those who are afraid of me, don't look me in the eyes or are up to some wrong, never like me. – Look at the black ones – then Orlov & Drenteln – Witte – *Kokovtzev* – *Trepov*, I feel it too – *Makarov* – *Kaufmann* – *Sofia Ivanovna* – *Mary* – *Sandra* Oblensky, etc., but those who are good & devoted to you honestly & purely – love me, – look at the simple people & military. The good & bad clergy its all so clear & therefore no more hurts me as when I was younger. Only when one allows oneself to write you or me nasty impertinent letters – you must punish.

Ania told me about *Balaschov* (the man I always disliked). I understood why you came so awfully late to bed & why I had such pain & anxiety writing. Please, Lovy, tell Frederiks to write him a strong *reprimand* (he & *Nicolai Mikhailovitch* & Vass make one in the club – he has such a high court-rank & dares to write, unasked. And its not the first time – in bygone days I remember he did so too. Tear up the letter, but have him firmly reprimanded – tell *Voyeikov* to remind the old man – such a smack to a conceited member of the Council of the Empire will be very useful.

We cannot now be trampled upon. Firmness above all! – Now you have made *Trepov's* son A.D.C. you can insist yet more on his working with *Protopopov*, he must prove his gratitude. – Remember to forbid *Gurko* speaking & mixing himself into politics – it ruined *Nikolasha* & Alexeiev, – the latter God sent this illness clearly to save you fr. a man who was losing his way & doing harm by listening to bad letters & people, instead of listening to yr. orders about the war & being obstinate. And one has set him against me – proof – what he said to old Ivanov. –

But soon all this things will blow over, its getting clearer & the weather too, which is a good sign, remember.

And our dear Friend is praying so hard for you – a man of God's near one gives the strength, faith & hope one needs so sorely. And others cannot understand this great calm of yours & therefore think you don't understand & try to ennervate, frighten & prick at you. But they will soon tire of it.

Should Mother dear write, remember the Michels are behind her. – Don't heed & take to heart – thank God, she is not here, but kind people find means of writing & doing harm. All is turning to the good – our Friends dreams mean so much. Sweety, go to the *Moghilev* Virgin & find peace and strength there – look in after tea, before you receive, take Baby with you, quietly – its so calm there – & you can place yr. candels. Let the people see you are a christian Sovereign & don't be shy – even such an example will help others. –

How will the lonely nights be? I cannot imagine it. The

consolation to hold you tightly clasped in my arms – it lulled the pain of soul & heart & I tried to put all my endless love, prayers & faith & strength into my caresses. So inexpressibly dear you are to me, husband of my heart. God bless you & my Baby treasure – I cover you with kisses; when sad, go to Baby's room & sit a bit quietly there with his nice people. Kiss the beloved child & you will feel warmed & calm. All my love I pour out to you, Sun of my life. –

Sleep well, heart & soul with you, my prayers around you – God & the holy Virgin will never forsake you –

Ever your very, very,

Own

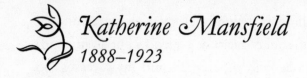

Katherine Mansfield
1888–1923

Katherine Mansfield was born Kathleen Beauchamp in Wellington, New Zealand, to parents of English descent. Her father was a successful self-made industrialist, and he and his wife were financially and socially ambitious. Kathleen was their third daughter; two more were followed by a son, Leslie.

In 1903 Katherine (she changed her name around this time) and her two older sisters were sent to Europe to be 'finished'; they attended a progressive school in London, where Katherine began a lifelong friendship with another pupil, Ida Baker, edited the school magazine and took holidays in Paris and Brussels. She returned to New Zealand in 1906, but agitated strongly to be allowed to go back to London. After she embarked on an affair with a young woman painter, her parents relented, and she left New Zealand for the last time in 1908.

The year following Katherine's arrival in London was chaotic, and had repercussions for the rest of her life. Having fallen in love with a fellow expatriate, a musician named Garnet Trowell, she joined a touring opera company (she was an accomplished cellist) in order to be with him, and became pregnant. On discovering this, she took off and married a respectable singing teacher ten years her senior named George Bowden. She fled immediately after the ceremony to take refuge with her friend Ida. Her mother came halfway around the world to investigate, and – having delivered a lecture to Ida's family on the dangers of lesbianism – whipped her off to a spa in Germany, where Katherine had a miscarriage. Mrs Beauchamp unceremoniously abandoned her there and returned to Wellington, where she promptly cut her daughter out of her will.

Katherine was able to return to London only after Ida paid her fare back from Germany. In the meantime, she had taken up with a Pole named Floryan Sobienowski, whom she was planning to marry in Paris. This plan seems to have been shelved when Katherine became seriously ill with untreated gonorrhoea, which left her requiring surgery and ended her chances of ever having a child.

One fruitful aspect of Katherine's enforced stay at the spa was a collection of stories, *In a German Pension*, which attracted some favourable attention when it was published in 1911, and led to her meeting John Middleton Murry, the editor of an avant-garde magazine named *Rhythm*. The two set up house together, after a fashion, and the next four years were spent flitting between London and Paris, dodging creditors, putting out the magazine and striking up friendships with a circle of writers and artists that included D. H. Lawrence and his lover, later wife, Frieda Weekley. Katherine did not produce any work during this time, and in 1915 left on her own for Paris, where she embarked on an affair with a French writer and began work on probably her most famous story, 'Prelude'. She returned to Murry in May. That October her brother Leslie, who had joined the army and was serving in France, was killed; the grieving Katherine insisted on travelling through the war-ravaged country, where Murry joined her shortly afterwards. A period of something approaching tranquillity and productive work in the south of France came to an end when the Lawrences summoned their friends to Zennor in Cornwall to take part in an experiment in communal living, which, somewhat predictably given the temperaments involved, lasted a matter of weeks.

Katherine was diagnosed with tuberculosis early in 1918 and went to France, accompanied by Ida, for treatment. She returned that March because her divorce from Bowden had finally come through and she and Murry were free to marry, which they did on 3 May. But the remaining years of Katherine's life were a blur of travel between London, France and Switzerland, as she attempted to stay one step ahead of the disease which she knew was killing her. She tried many treatments, some undeniably quackish, some straightforwardly harmful, and finally came to rest at an establishment at Fontainebleau, outside Paris, run by a Greek-Armenian guru. On 9 January 1923, Murry was permitted to visit her there; she died the same evening.

Murry became the guardian of her manuscripts, and for the twenty years after her death devoted himself to editing and publishing the letters, journals, stories and poems she had left behind, securing her reputation as one of the most influential writers of the early twentieth century (and not doing badly out of the proceeds, it must be said; Ida Baker, after years of devoted friendship, received nothing).

The first three letters below date from Katherine's stay in Paris after she began an affair with a French writer. Seen in that context, they are fascinating in their apparent neediness – presumably Katherine had realized by then that she wanted to return home. The final letter here is not a love letter, but demonstrates her method for dealing with rivals for her husband's affections. Even now, its icy condescension is quite terrifying.

To John Middleton Murry
Sent from Paris, 19 March 1915

Very strange is my love for you tonight. Don't have it psycho-analysed. I saw you suddenly lying in a hot bath, blinking up at me – your charming beautiful body half under the water. I sat on the edge of the bath in my vest waiting to come in. Everything in the room was wet with steam and it was night-time and you were rather languid. 'Tig, chuck over that sponge.' No, I'll *not* think of you like that. I'll shut my teeth and not listen to my heart. It begins to cry as if it were a child in an empty room and to beat on the door and say 'Jack – Jack – Jack and Tig.' I'll be better when I've had a letter.

Ah, my God, how can I love him like this! Do I love you so much more than you love me or do you too . . . feel like this?

TIG

Saturday morning. Just off to see if there are any letters. I'm all right, dearest.

To John Middleton Murry, 26 March 1915

Dearest darling,

I'm in such a state of worry and suspense that I can't write to you tonight or send you anything. When I came back from the fruitless search for letters the concierge began a long story about an Alsatian in the house who had received yesterday a four-page letter for the name of Bowden.* 'Another came today,' said she, 'I gave it back to the post-man.' I literally screamed. I have *written* this name for her and she'd utterly forgotten it, thinking of me only as Mans-field. Since then I've simply rushed from post-office to post-office. The Alsatian is out. I'm waiting for her and the postman now. My heart dies in my breast with terror at the thought of a letter of yours being lost. I simply don't exist. I suppose I exaggerate – but I'd plunge into the Seine – or lie on a railway line – rather than lose a letter. You know, bogey, my heart is simply crying all the time and I am fright-ened, desolate, useless for anything.

Oh, my precious – my beloved little Jag, forgive Tig such a silly scrawl.

But life ought not to do such things to you and me. I could *kill* the concierge – yes, with pleasure. 'Une lettre d'Angleterre dans un couvert bleu.'

Courage! But at this moment I am simply running as fast as I can and crying my loudest into your arms.

I will write you properly tomorrow. This is just to say that I love you and that you are the breath of life to me.

Tig

* Katherine's married name

To John Middleton Murry, 28 March 1915

Jack, I shan't hide what I feel today. I woke up with you in my breast and on my lips. Jack, I love you terribly today. The whole world is gone. There is only you. I walk about, dress, eat, write – but all the time I am *breathing* you. Time and again I have been on the point of telegraphing you that I am coming home as soon as Kay sends my money. It is still possible that I shall.

> *Jack, Jack, I want to come back,*
> *And to hear the little ducks go*
> *Quack! Quack! Quack!*

Life is too short for our love even though we stayed together every moment of all the years. I cannot think of you – our life – our darling life – you, my treasure – everything about you.

No, no, no. Take me quickly into your arms. Tig is a tired girl and she is crying. I want you, I want you. Without you life is nothing.

Your woman
Tig

To John Middleton Murry
Sent from 24 Redcliffe Road, Fulham, Saturday night,
18 May 1917

My darling

Do not imagine, because you find these lines in your private book that I have been trespassing. You know I have not – and where else shall I leave a love letter? For I long to write you a love letter tonight. You are all about me – I seem to breathe you – hear you – feel you in me and of me – What am I doing here? You are away – I have seen you in the train, at the station, driving up, sitting in the lamplight talking, greeting people – washing your hands – And I am here – in your tent – sitting at your table. There are some wallflower petals on the table and a dead match, a blue pencil and a *Magdeburgische Zeitung*. I am just as much at home as they.

When dusk came – flowing up the silent garden – lapping against the blind windows – my first & last terror started up – I was making some coffee in the kitchen. It was so violent, so dreadful I put down the coffee-pot – and simply ran away – ran out of the studio and up the street with my bag under one arm and a block of writing paper and a pen under the other. I felt that if I could get here & find Mrs [illegible] I should be 'safe' – I found her and I lighted your gas, wound up your clock – drew your curtains – & embraced your black overcoat before I sat down – frightened no longer. Do not be angry with me, Bogey – ca a ete plus fort que moi . . . That is why I am here.

When you came to tea this afternoon you took a brioche broke it in half & padded the inside doughy bit with two fingers. You always do that with a bun or a roll or a piece of bread – It is your way – your head a little on one side the while . . .

When you opened your suitcase I saw your old feltie and a French book and a comb all higgledy piggledy – 'Tig. I've only got 3 handkerchiefs' – Why should that memory be so sweet to me? . . .

Last night, there was a moment before you got into bed. You stood, quite naked, bending forward a little – talking. It was only for an instant. I saw you – I loved you so – loved your body with such tenderness – Ah my dear – And I am not thinking now of 'passion'. No, of that other thing that makes me feel that every inch of you is so precious to me. Your soft shoulders – your creamy warm skin, your ears, cold like shells are cold – your long legs and your feet that I love to clasp with my feet – the feeling of your belly – & your thin young back – Just below that bone that sticks out at the back of your neck you have a little mole. It is partly because we are young that I feel this tenderness – I love your youth – I could not bear that it should be touched even by a cold wind if I were the Lord.

We two, you know have everything before us, and we shall do very great things – I have perfect faith in us – and so perfect is my love for you that I am, as it were, still, silent to my very soul. I want nobody but you for my lover and my friend and to nobody but you shall I be *faithful*.

I am yours for ever.

Tig

To John Middleton Murry, Sunday night, 27 January 1918

My love and my darling,

It is ten minutes past eight. I must tell you how much I love you at ten minutes past eight on a Sunday evening, January 27th 1918.

I have been indoors all day (except for posting your letter) and I feel greatly rested. Juliette has come back from a new excursion into the country, with blue irises – do you remember how beautifully they grew in that little house with the trellis tower round by the rocks? – and all sorts and kinds of sweet-smelling jonquils . . . The room is very warm. I have a handful of fire, and the few little flames dance on the log and can't make up their minds to attack it . . . There goes a train. Now it is quiet again except for my watch. I look at the minute hand and think what a spectacle I shall make of myself when I am really coming home to you. How I shall sit in the railway carriage, and put the old watch in my lap and pretend to cover it with a book – but not read or see, but just whip it up with my longing gaze, and simply make it go faster.

My love for you tonight is so deep and tender that it seems to be outside myself as well. I am fast shut up like a little lake in the embrace of some big mountains, you would see me down below, deep and shining – and quite fathomless, my dear. You might drop your heart into me and you'd never hear it touch bottom. I love you – I love you – Goodnight.

Oh, Bogey, what it is to love like this!

To Princess Bibesco (née Elizabeth Asquith, 1897–1945, daughter of Herbert Asquith and Margot Tennant, married to a Romanian diplomat twenty-two years her senior), 24 March 1921

Dear Princess Bibesco,

I am afraid you must stop writing these little love letters to my husband while he and I live together. It is one of the things which is not done in our world.

You are very young. Won't you ask your husband to explain to you the impossibility of such a situation.

Please do not make me have to write to you again. I do not like scolding people and I simply hate having to teach them manners.

Yours sincerely,
Katherine Mansfield

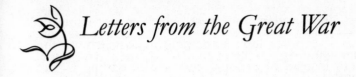

Letters from the Great War

The First World War raged from 1914 to 1918, and was the first truly global war in history, with fronts in Europe, the Middle East, Africa and Asia. The casualty figures are devastating: one in three British families had a loved one killed, wounded or taken prisoner. The letters below from a woman in Walthamstow to her soldier husband, remarkable for their brightness and bravery, give a tiny insight into what life was like for those left behind.

Walthamstow E17, 17 September 1916

My Dearest one and only,
Oh for the sight of your dear face, I feel it more everyday, it seems years since you were here and took dear Baby and I in your arms and when I look out and see the pouring rain my heart feels fit to break to think of you in the cold dismal tent, while I am at home with a nice fire. Oh dear it does seem terrible to me and you've done nothing to deserve it. Sunday seems the same as every day but worse today it's the 17th dear. Well dear matey I have sent this parcel and hope you will like them, they are plain this time and also

kerchieves and another undervest, which in unfolding be careful, as I've put a little something in to celebrate the anniversery instead of sending cigs – Well darling I can't think of any more new just now but let me know if anything you are needing, by the way would you like a couple of pig's bladders to fill your breeches out, they'd make fine cushions as well, that's the worst of these cheap bums. Heaps of love and kisses from your dear little Baby and everloving devoted wifie

25 June 1917

My Own dear Hubby,
Your dear letter of Sat. just received – Well darling mine I have just a little news to tell you which I'm sure you will regret to hear. Poor Harry Saville has gone under, news have just come through that he was shot on the 10th & died of his wounds on the 15th & they never had notice he was wounded even, so it was a terrible shock to them, poor Mrs S. is properly knocked over & Mrs Styles son lays at Bournemouth badly wounded from France. Oh darling it seems so terrible if only it would end and send you back to me. I should know you were safe, it seems ages & ages since your dear face was before me & when one hears bad news it makes you feels so downhearted – Excuse this scrawl as I've got Baby in my arms asleep and it's rather difficult – Cheer up sweetheart all my dearest love to you darling & heaps of kisses from your dear little treasure who says

daddy's gone to fight the naughty shermans & she wont love em. Your everloving everlonging & devoted to you wife and Babs

5 November 1917

My own dearest one,
At last thank God I have heard from you, from Durban dated Sept 19 & 20 & one posted at sea all 3 arrived together on 30 october & silk hanky as well, after long weary months of waiting my patients were rewarded & thanks awfully darling it was so sweet of you, to see your dear writing once more was like a hidden treasure. What an experience for you dearest & what a lot you will have to tell dear babby & I when you return to us again, & how many an evening we shall sit in the dear firelight listening to all your travels. What a time that will be dear, one can hardly realise it, if only it was for some other purpose, one could be so very much happier, but there dear that's the way of this wicked war, so I must buck up for your dear sake, & we will make up for all this when you come back to us which I pray please God will not be much longer now as we are all fed up with it – And your sweet little daughter joins me with all our dearest, best & devoted love to you dear & lots of loving kisses, & hope you will come safely home to us soon.

The following sources were invaluable:

Love in Letters Illustrated in the Correspondence of Eminent Persons with Biographical Sketches of the Writers by Allan Grant, G. W. Carleton & Co., New York, 1867

Love Letters of Famous Men and Women, J. T. Merydew (ed.), Remington & Co., London, 1888

Love Affairs of Famous Men & Women, Henri Pène du Bois (ed.), Gibbings & Company, London, 1900

Love Letters of Famous People, Freeman Bunting (ed.), Gay and Bird, London, 1907

Letters of Love, Arthur L. Humphreys, London, 1911

Love Letters of Great Men and Women, C. H. Charles (ed.), Stanley Paul & Co, London, 1924

Love Letters: An Anthology from the British Isles, 975–1944, James Turner (ed.), Cassell & Company Ltd, London, 1970

Love Letters, Antonia Fraser (ed.), Weidenfeld & Nicolson, London, 1976

The Virago Book of Love Letters, Jill Dawson (ed.), Virago Press Ltd, London, 1994

Love Letters, Peter Washington (ed.), Everyman's Library, London, 1996

The Virago Book of Women and the Great War, Joyce Marlow (ed.), Virago Press Ltd., London, 1998

The Massachusetts Historical Society online archive,
www.masshist.org

Project Gutenberg, www.gutenberg.org

Acknowledgements

Thanks to JB and JG and my friends at Pan Macmillan. Thanks to LG and UM and my friends at Little, Brown. Thanks to my family, immediate and extended, great men and women all. Thanks to the staff at the British Library. And thanks above all to DP, runner of support services, van man supreme, best beloved.

A note on the type

This book is set in Monotype Garamond, an old-style serif typeface prized for its consistency and fluency. The original 'Garamond' was the work of the fifteenth-century punch-cutter Claude Garamond, whose lower-case letters were in turn inspired by the handwriting of Angelo Vergecio, librarian to King Francis I of France. A twentieth-century vogue for recutting historical typefaces lead to a rash of 'Garamond' letterforms, from Stempel Garamond to Granjon and Sabon. In 1926, however, it was revealed that other new members of the Garamond 'family', such as Monotype Garamond, were actually based on the work of a later punch-cutter called Jean Jannon.